THE Fun
of Being
Looney

Bishop Richard Looney

Foreword by Charles Maynard

CITY ROAD
PUBLISHING

A Division of Market Square Books

The Fun of Being Looney

©2021 Richard Looney

books@marketsquarebooks.com
P.O. Box 23664   Knoxville, Tennessee 37933

ISBN: 978-1-950899-37-1

Printed and Bound in the United States of America

Cover Illustration & Book Design ©2021 City Road Books

City Road Books is a division of:
Market Square Publishing, LLC

Editor: Sheri Carder Hood
Publisher: Kevin Slimp

Table of Contents

Foreword

Never could I have imagined, upon first meeting Richard Looney, what a bright thread in the tapestry of my life he would be. I was a high school student attending a district youth event at the church where Richard was pastor. We met in the parking lot. At the time, I was six feet tall, which was tall for a person my age. I had gone to the event with my pastor, who was considerably shorter than me. As a youth, I was accustomed to being one of the tallest people in the room. However, when I met the formidable Richard Looney, I was awed just by his height. Then I heard that deep, rumbling voice. Surely God's voice sounded like this!

It appeared to be a chance encounter in a church parking lot. Months later, I saw him at a district conference—not hard to spot him in a crowd! Then I was off to Emory & Henry, Richard's alma mater also.

My first Sunday as a freshman, I attended worship at Emory UMC, the campus church. A gathering for new students was announced for that evening as a chance for new students to meet people of the Emory community. I went for the free non-cafeteria food! Some professors and their spouses were there as well as people who lived in Emory. At one point, the pastor asked us to find a partner and introduce ourselves. I stood there for a moment and a rather tall, muscular, older man came up to me. "Hello, I'm Carl." I introduced myself as Charles from Chattanooga. "Oh," he said. "Chattanooga! Do you know my son, Richard Looney? He served White Oak in Chattanooga." Richard Looney, the tall pastor in the parking lot!

Richard's parents, Carl and Ruth Looney, became a wonderful part of my life at college. Their hospitality to students—and everyone, for that matter—was warm and loving. They worked tirelessly for many causes in numerous and creative ways.

When I was in seminary, Richard became the district superintendent of my home district, and I reported to the District Committee on Ministry under his direction. When I was ordained a deacon, Richard Looney was one of the first people to congratulate me. Little did I know that I would be hearing from him sooner rather than later.

At Christmastime in my middle year at Candler, I was visiting my parents. One evening my mother answered the phone and said, "Yes, he's right here." She handed me the phone and mouthed, It's the district superintendent. I whispered, "What does he want?" She proffered the phone with a shrug.

"Hello, this is Charles."

"Charles, this is Richard Looney," rumbled the deep voice on the other end. Surely God's voice sounds like this, I thought again. "Charles, I have a situation that I need some help with. Would you consider…"

Richard laid out that New Salem UMC on Lookout Mountain in Dade County, Georgia, needed a pastor immediately. There had been a series of unfortunate circumstances, and the church needed a pastor posthaste.

"You can serve the church on the weekends and continue your studies at Candler. If you will do this for six months, then we will appoint someone full time at conference in June."

I got more particulars, and we agreed to talk the next day. I had been a student pastor while at Emory & Henry but had decided not to serve a church while in seminary. My wife, Janice, and I talked about it and felt that we could help. After all, it was only for six months. When we talked the next day, Richard told me that his first appointment while at Candler was also in Dade County, down at Rising Fawn. He knew people in the New Salem church and assured me that we would love them.

I began at New Salem on a snowy Sunday in January. The second weekend we were there, Mrs. Baker, the matriarch of one of the leading families at New Salem—who was also related to most of the congregation—was taken to the hospital in Chattanooga. I knew that I needed to visit her, but I had to return to Atlanta. That afternoon I called my district superintendent and reported the situation and then asked him to make a hospital visit for me. It never occurred to me that I should not have imposed on the DS to do my job. He told me that he would gladly do it. Only when I was in school that week and recounting this to a friend did I hear, "You've got to be kidding! Please tell me you did not ask Rev. Looney to visit!"

When conference arrived, I was appointed to another year at New Salem while Richard was appointed to Munsey and left the Chattanooga District. "Only six months" turned into five-and-a-half wonderful years in Dade County.

Our paths continued to cross over the years. In 1988, it was with pride and sadness that I read of Richard's election to the episcopacy. It was wonderful that he was elected. We all knew the United Methodist Church was adding a good bishop, but I was sorry to see him leave Holston. Even though we had only had a few conversations over the years, I realized that I was going to miss his presence. After twelve years with the South Georgia Conference, Richard retired.

Upon his retirement, Bishop Looney began working for the Foundation for Evangelism at Lake Junaluska. He worked to raise funds to support evangelism throughout the United Methodist connection, particularly for chairs of evangelism at the UMC seminaries. Our acquaintance grew into friendship as he asked me to tell stories at the Foundation for Evangelism dinner at Lake Junaluska while I was involved in fundraising at the International Storytelling Center in Jonesborough, Tennessee. We swapped notes, ideas, and above all, stories.

Richard's service record only tells part of his story, but it does show his influence in local churches, the Holston Conference, and throughout the connection. He has attended ten of the thirteen General Conferences since the inception of the United Methodist Church. Even his retirement from "active" service did not slow him down or bring him to inactivity.

- 1957 -1961
  Rising Fawn Circuit, Dade County, Georgia

- 1961-1964
  Baker's Chapel-Wyndale, Abingdon, Virginia

- 1964-1968
  Pleasant View (formerly Baker's Chapel), Abingdon, Virginia

- 1968-1972
  White Oak, Chattanooga, Tennessee

- 1972-1976
  Broad Street, Cleveland, Tennessee

- 1976-1979
  Chattanooga District, Chattanooga, Tennessee

- 1979-1987
  Munsey Memorial, Johnson City, Tennessee

- 1987-1988
  Church Street, Knoxville, Tennessee

- 1988-2000
  Bishop, South Georgia Conference, Macon, Georgia, Area

- Retired in 2000.
  Served for eight years as episcopal director of the Foundation for Evangelism, Lake Junaluska, North Carolina.

- 2009-2012
  Telford UMC, Telford, Tennessee

- 2013-2014
  Munsey Memorial, Johnson City, Tennessee

- 2016-2017   Church Street, Knoxville, Tennessee

- Delegate from Holston Conference to General
  Conference – 1980, 1984, 1988

- Attended General Conference as bishop – 1992, 1996,
  2000, 2004, 2008, 2012, 2016

After Bishop Looney re-retired, he came to Telford
UMC just outside of Jonesborough. We began getting
together for lunch at the Main Street Café. I reveled in
hearing his stories: his days in Dade County where we
had both served, his travels as a bishop, his bicycle trip
around Great Britain and Europe. For every question
I had, he answered with a story. Often I would ask
for a repeat of "The Best of the Fun of Being Looney."
He kindly listened to my own Dade stories and other
tales. Growing up in Appalachia, as we both did, we
swapped tall tales and folk stories as well. Many of our
conversations/sessions began with, "Have you heard
the one about...?" or "Tell the one about...!"

We often spoke at the same events, particularly
Holston's Jubilation each year. I once involved him
in a sermon in which we both removed our shoes to
determine if the feet of those who preach the gospel
are truly beautiful—certainly a theological question
of weight. What big feet the man has!!! Only a friend
would play along with that request!

A few years later, Janice and I went on a trip to England and Scotland with professors and students from Tennessee Wesleyan. It was a wonderful experience seeing the land of Wordsworth, Coleridge, Scott, Burns, Whitfield, and the Wesleys. One Sunday we attended worship at the Methodist church in Keswick in the Lake District. The congregation warmly welcomed us and served us tea afterwards. A woman came up to me and said, "I understand that you are from Tennessee."

"Yes, ma'am."

"We once had a pastor for a season who came to us by way of an exchange program. Our pastor went to Tennessee, and we had a delightful fellow from there. I wondered if you might know him."

"What is his name?"

"I cannot remember exactly. He was a rather tall fellow with a wonderful smile who told us many stories. I believe he became a bishop."

"Richard Looney???"

"Why, yes, certainly! Richard Looney!"

Even in the Lake District of England, I crossed Richard's path! His friendships encircle the globe.

Our friendship has continued through the years. Again in retirement, he served as interim pastor at

Munsey and Church Street. I kept trying to get a lunch with him when I could. "There is a good Chinese place in South Knoxville." Sold! I was there with the usual, "Tell me about going to…" "Have you heard the one about…?"

I was thrilled when he told me of this book. It is a chance to sit down at lunch with him again. Only now you, the reader, can join in on The Fun of Being Looney.

Charles W. Maynard
Knoxville, Tennessee 2021

Introduction

There is no nobler calling than the ministry. We, as pastors, interact with peoples' lives at their highest and lowest moments. We point beyond ourselves to God and seek to be a bridge between the human and divine. While our work is serious and life-changing, we can never take ourselves too seriously. In fact, the load of ministry might be too heavy to bear without the ability to laugh at oneself and with colleagues.

It is freeing to realize that Jesus must have laughed heartily. One of my favorite paintings, in fact, is of the laughing Jesus. People loved to be in his company. A professor reminded his students to learn to enjoy preaching because people are unlikely to come regularly to church to watch someone suffer. People flocked to Jesus to share in the joy he exhibited.

Think of the humorous way Jesus critiques the

religious leaders and others of his day. One was so eager to be noticed that he hired a trumpet player to announce a large gift. Others loved to pray piously on the street corners to be seen and applauded. Still others sought seats up front where everyone would surely notice. If it is recognition you want, that will be your reward.

Or picture the nitpicker trying to remove a speck from his neighbor's eye, unaware that a log is protruding from his own; or imagine a rich person having as much difficulty getting into heaven as a camel—hump and long legs—trying to get through the eye of a needle. We have so elevated the divine Jesus that we have forgotten the humor of Jesus, who was accused of being a party animal and friend of sinners and who laughingly reminded them of the absurdity of criticizing a doctor for associating with sick people.

For some reason, I have been given the kind of mind that can see and remember the humorous in my own life and in my service to the church. Some of that, I choose to share here, hoping that you will discover the humor in your own life and circumstances. Maybe our joy will attract others to the joy given by Christ.

Years ago, I heard Lee Rippey describe the testimony meetings of his youth. An older brother would stand and say in a somber voice, "I've been serving the Lord for fifty years—been up, been down, pray for me." A dear sister would say, "I've been serving the Lord for forty years. It's been hard, pray for me." After thirty minutes of such heavy testimony, the leaders invited the young people forward to "get" what their elders had gotten. The youth, however, would escape as quickly as possible after the invitation because life was simply too exciting now to give up for what they had just heard. Forgive us, Lord, if we have turned your joy into heaviness.

The Fun of Being Looney

Over the years, I have discovered that life can be fun and is surely funny. With the last name Looney, one can laugh about it or become touchy. It has become easier and easier to laugh, however, and enjoy the humor found in strange places, circumstances, and people.

The Looney name provides many occasions for laughter, especially when combined with other unusual names. For example, as a young pastor, I was assigned to preach in an adjoining annual conference as part of an exchange program whereby each church welcomed a visiting pastor. The owner of the local motel where we stayed thought we were putting him on when Eddie Fox, John Duck, W.I. Farmer, and Richard Looney checked in the same afternoon.

During my retirement, I worked with the Foundation for Evangelism, located at Lake Junaluska, North

Carolina. Two other unusual names made an amusing trio: Looney, Crook, and Cannon. Over the years, I came to be renamed "Looney Tunes."

One of my staff members at the time, Rev. McDonald, was doing some work at the psychiatric clinic in Chattanooga. Without thinking one day, I called to speak to Rev. McDonald, identifying myself as Richard Looney. "Who?" the receptionist asked. Then I had to spell it. After a long wait, a staff person came on laughing heartily. My name had caused great suspicion; maybe I was a disgruntled husband wanting to confront the counselor who had given unwelcome advice. A similar story was repeated with my dad when we visited Washington and Lee University near Lexington, Virginia. The custodian shared the account of four students who were stopped on suspicion of drunk driving. Each of them happened to be the namesake of a famous Virginia politician, leader, or jurist: Robert E. Lee, Robert Byrd, Jr., Carter Glass, and Fred Vinson. The officer calmly pushed his hat back and announced that he was Napoleon Bonaparte and would now like their real names.

After my election to the episcopacy, I liked to say that I was the first Looney elected a bishop. My friends reminded me that we had elected several looneys, but I was the first with the name to match.

Tall Tales

My size elicits stares and prompts the usual questions about "the weather up there" or "did you play basketball?" I am amused to be noticed, but not every tall person is so pleased. When asked the usual question about basketball, one tall man asked his short questioner if he was a jockey.

Our family loved to tease, and it was taken in stride for we knew we were loved. Dad was particularly adept at keeping us in our place. I had a sudden growth spurt between 12 and 15, reaching 6'6" by 15. He informed me that I grew so tall because there was no weight between my ears.

My unusual growth spurt led to some humorous occasions. At age 13, I wore a size 13 shoe; at 14, a size 14 shoe. Such were almost impossible to find. Mother began ordering my shoes from King Size in Brockton,

Massachusetts, when I was 13.

One day I had gone with Dad to Bluefield, West Virginia, where he was to make hospital calls. He spotted a well-known men's store and said, "Boy, let's have a little fun." As we entered the store, he asked, "This is a men's store, is it not?"

The clerk answered, "Yes, sir, and the finest in West Virginia."

"Good," said my dad. "My boy needs a pair of shoes."

"Fine," said the clerk. "What size?"

"Fourteen D" was the reply.

"Sorry, sir, we don't carry that size," answered the clerk.

So, Dad announced in his finest pulpit voice, "You should take down the men's store sign, for you can't outfit a 14-year-old boy." I was amused but a bit embarrassed.

At Emory & Henry College, my friends teased me by saying the Lord had created the earth, and Dick Looney was trying to cover it up. When I joined the Hermesian Literary Society on campus, I soon had to give an extemporaneous speech. I was called forward, handed a topic, and expected to begin speaking. My topic, "The Advantages of Big Feet." I talked for a short time and was seated. I would have guessed it to be a two-minute talk, but I talked for seven. There were apparently more advantages than I realized.

In my second appointment, I was making a pastoral call on an older member whose grandchildren were visiting from out of state. A little boy kept staring at my feet. Finally, he said, "Preacher, why are you wearing clown shoes?" I had a hardy laugh, but the grandmother was embarrassed.

Having grown up in West Virginia, I pay particular attention to the state's stories. A young, 7'6" basketball prospect was being courted by every college and university in the state. With his height and agility, he would change a program overnight. Finally, he was persuaded to fill out a generic application form. For "birth date," he wrote "January 1, January 2, and January 3."

The Early Years

Looking back on my life, the humorous and ironic began quite early. I was the firstborn of Carl and Ruth Looney. My dad was a gifted pastor and preacher; my mother, a devoted wife and Christian, gifted in many ways for home and church. I was due in March, but after my mother had a hard fall, I was born on February 14 at home before the arrival of the doctor. I had difficulty breathing, and they feared for my life.

Their earnest prayers were answered with my early improvement, and a robust son grew to be 6'6" and played football and basketball. I enjoy saying that I would have been a "real man" had I been carried full term. Later, the parsonage was sold to make way for a supermarket. For a boy—and man—with a ceaseless appetite, a grocery store is a fitting monument to Carl and Ruth's firstborn.

My recollections of school provide many happy, funny memories. I began school at Leemaster Elementary, two miles from our residence. On the walk to school, I was joined by others along the way, and we had fun traipsing to school in a small army. At that time, one teacher taught several grades within the same room, and the older students worked with the younger students in a cloak room.

My early education was accelerated because I learned to read before beginning school. Mother had started a library for the mountain community in our home with discarded books from larger libraries. So, I passed to third grade my first year. During Christmas of my first year, I announced to my dad that one of the boys told me that there was no Santa Claus. "What did you do?" asked Dad. "I whipped him" was my reply. That week we went for a long trek in the woods hunting for squirrels. Deep in the woods, we sat on a log, and I learned the sad truth.

I later attended school in Grundy, Virginia. Our teacher had a novel idea for punishment. She had a wooden paddle, but the offending pupil had to bend over and administer his own paddling. One boy, who was frequently bent over before the class, would yell with each lick, however slight. Our teacher had a knack, though, for knowing if there was real pain.

Growing up, we lived on a small mountain farm in Southwest Virginia while Dad traveled as an evangelist. Building houses, growing crops, and tending animals was part of my life as was cutting timber and working around a sawmill. One of the millers had a violent temper and caused real amusement when he threw his hat at the large circular saw only to see it chewed to bits.

I enjoyed teasing my beloved dog by putting my hand under the sawdust and moving it slightly so he would dig frantically for this unseen creature. We cleared brush around the farm's apple orchard regularly and hauled rocks each summer from a field that seemed to produce them in abundance. We picked berries, strung fence, harvested crops, and generally shared the life of hardworking farmers. The hills were so steep that we laughed about needing mules with legs longer on one side.

We moved from Virginia to West Virginia. Because West Virginia had twelve grades and Virginia had only eleven, it was customary to move the transferring student forward one grade. With this event, I managed to graduate high school at age sixteen.

High school was a fulfilling time. Elkhorn High School in Switchback, West Virginia, was small in enrollment but had a wonderful core of teachers and an amazing variety of electives. I played football, performed in the school band, and sang in the school chorus. I learned to cut stencils and run a mimeograph machine, which helped greatly in my first pastoral appointment where I was pastor and secretary.

Dad and I had a major argument over my course choices. I wanted to take chemistry, but he insisted I take typing. I lost that argument but have been forever grateful. Typing was most helpful in college, in seminary, and in the ministry. Even today, my computer work is enhanced by that training.

Our high school was a wonderful mixture of students from immigrant families connected to the coal mines. There were parents from Hungary, Italy, Poland, and others. One of my band buddies was a rounder. He brought his first report card home full of F's and D's; his sister had A's and B's. The boy explained to his father that he didn't understand America yet: F was for fine, D for dandy, A was awful, and B bad. Only the intervention of the mother saved the daughter from a whipping.

Our principal was a stern taskmaster and had been nicknamed after a prison warden in a movie. He was so tight that it was rumored he went out on Christmas Eve, fired his pistol in the air, and then told his daughter that someone had shot Santa so there would be no Christmas that year.

With all his sternness, I helped bring humor to his office one day. One of my good buddies was named Billy. I was the largest guy in school and extremely timid. Billy was the smallest—almost a dwarf—but full of bluster. One day the librarian, who was also the principal's wife, sent both of us to the principal's office: I happened to be sitting quietly at the table where Billy was showing forth. When we walked in, the principal had to stifle a laugh. Billy strutted in as if he owned the place. I was obviously scared stiff. He sent us out for a moment to compose himself and then tried to administer a stern warning. It was obvious that the contrast in our demeanor was about to break him up.

Our French teacher sought to instill a bit of class in us, offering a grade elevation if we would wear a tie. We missed the point, however. We stuffed our ties into our pockets and pulled them out before her class. Somehow a tie with a flannel shirt and jeans looked comical rather than classy.

My first paying job was in the company store of a large coal company. I cleared very little money since the distance required room and board. I did, however, gain a wealth of experience with the hardworking miners and regular customers. The miners called me long distance and kept me amused by their regular clever humor, even in the midst of grim working conditions.

When someone asked to have their groceries put on credit, the clerks slipped into a hall and called the office to verify the customer's credibility. On one occasion, it was necessary to re-shelve a large order because credit was denied. The order was refilled two hours later when the customer returned with cash. On another occasion, laughter erupted when I called to verify a gentleman's credibility. Yes, his credit was fine; he happened to be the president of the company.

It is often assumed that ministers live sheltered lives shut off from the experiences of common life. I grew up in a minister's home and have been a minister since my early twenties. But even so, I have shared the lives of people in many varied circumstances.

One summer I worked with the city water company digging ditches with a pick and a shovel. The project started with a crew of eleven, nine of whom were ex-convicts. I heard language daily that shocked the sensibilities. One day the police arrived to report neighborhood complaints about the profanity. While I never used such language, the police directed their words at me. After their departure, the fellows suggested, with chuckles, that they continue their profanity so the preacher's boy could be locked up.

In spite of the rough edges, we developed a real appreciation for one another. I later heard some words quoted from an old ditch-digger that have been an inspiration over the years: "I can dig a ditch so straight and true that God himself can see it through."

In Dad's second appointment, the bishop and district superintendent stopped by the parsonage for a surprise visit. During the visit, Mom and Dad realized, to their horror, that I had seated myself on top of the bishop's impressive Hamburg hat. Fortunately, the bishop had a sense of humor and later remembered the incident fondly. Our son, David, paid me back in kind when my bishop stopped for a visit. He gave each of the children a 50-cent piece. Instead of saying, "Thank you," David said, "I'll have another of these, please."

I have a younger sister, Betty, and an even younger brother, David. We had a great deal of fun growing up together. David picked up several songs, including, "Pistol Packin' Mama." One Sunday, the Sunday school superintendent asked for a volunteer to sing a song, and David immediately offered to do so. Our mother turned pale, only to breathe a deep sigh of relief when he began to sing, "Jesus Loves Me, This I Know."

On another occasion, David found a cigarette butt with which to play. Mother spotted him, so he took off circling the house with Mother after him. Picture a tall mother chasing a short, dumpy, little boy. Finally, he darted in the house and was properly disciplined.

David reported the next morning that he dreamed a frightening scene: his mother had become a bear. So, upon hearing this, my sensitive mother had a good cry. In fact, she cried when she was happy as well as sad. Sometimes when we observed her crying, we would ask, "Should we be happy or sad?"

My sister, Betty, did not like to be rushed when she was young and created many a crisis as we tried to urge her on, lest she miss the school bus. In spite of raising her own three wonderful children, her pace has seldom quickened. Recently during our weekly phone chat, I asked how she was doing, and she replied that she was having to slow down. I reminded her that such an occurrence was not possible. She laughed harder than I.

At age 12, I joined the Scout troop in Maybeury, West Virginia. The troop folded a month later, so my father enrolled me as a Lone Scout. I spent the summers at Camp Roland in Bland County, Virginia, and eventually achieved the rank of Eagle. Because of my size, I was soon a counselor serving as bugler, lifeguard, and archery instructor. Training as a scout had a profoundly positive influence on my life and development, and it also provided some humorous memories. Once, a younger scout went underwater during a test swim across the river or creek. I dived in to rescue him. After reaching him, I realized we were not in over my head, and instead of swimming out, I walked out with him. "The Lifeguard Who Couldn't Swim" became a tale often repeated.

As bugler, I was too visible for comfort: greatly appreciated at mess call, but much resented for *Taps*— lights out—and immensely despised for *Reveille*. I often had the following sung to me:

> *Oh, how we hate to get up in the morning,*
> *Oh, how we'd rather remain in bed,*
> *The cruelest blow of all is to hear the bugler call,*
> *You gotta get up, you gotta get up in the morning.*
> *Someday we're gonna murder the bugler –*
> *Someday they're gonna find him dead.*
> *We'll amputate his reveille and sit upon it heavily*
> *And spend the rest of our days in bed.*
> *Then we'll get the other pup,*
> *The guy that wakes the bugler up,*
> *And spend the rest of our days in bed.*

We even sang a parody for mess call:

> *"Soupy, soupy, soupy, without a single bean,*
> *Bacon, bacon, bacon, without a bit of lean,*
> *Coffee, coffee, coffee, without a bit of cream."*

The sound of *Taps* on the bugle still haunts me and is especially inspiring at the close of a committal service:

Day is done, gone the sun, from the lake, from the hills, from the sky. All is well, safely rest, God is nigh.

I read recently that Sir Winston Churchill had requested Taps be played at his funeral service; then, after a moment of silence, Reveille be sounded. "You gotta get up, you gotta get up, you gotta get up in the morning."

With our assurance of resurrection, it can even be fun to plan one's own funeral. The God who is with us in life is with us through death.

The Joy of Music

Music was an important part of our family life. Mother played the piano and Dad sang. In addition, Dad taught himself to play the trumpet and violin. In time, I played the trumpet and sang in the choir; Betty Ruth played the piano and flute; and David played the trumpet and sang. Many evenings found us singing around the piano as a family.

The three Looney men sang specials during church and revival services. Dad would make an exaggerated production of placing his boys on a lower step so we would be even. David was 6'4 1/2", I was 6'6", and Dad was 6'1". This placement usually brought a murmur of laughter from the congregation.

Music continues to enrich and inspire my life. Reading and study go better with classical music in the background, and the experience of music provides some happy and funny memories.

In high school, I sang bass in the school quartet. We had invitations to sing at a variety of events, including a Catholic church. We had a jazzed-up, boogie rendition of Jingle Bells ready to perform. To our horror, though, upon arrival at the church, we discovered we were to be singing in the sanctuary rather than the fellowship hall. With no other number prepared for the season, we escaped by slowing down the boogie beat about four times.

Dad loved to sing "The Ninety and Nine," and he had a strong, resonant voice. While conducting a revival in the panhandle of West Virginia, a farmer asked him to sing again one night. In a teasing way, Dad said he would do it for a goat—in that region, farmers kept a rare breed of goat prized for their milk. The man said, "Go ahead." Several months later, Dad received notice that he was to pick up his goat at the train station. He was embarrassed, for he had only been teasing. Our goat was a nanny expecting a kid. In due time, a billy goat was born and became a useful part of Dad's visits to schools where children flocked around this proud, prancing show-off.

Over the years, I sang with the choirs in the churches I served as I found that to be a wonderful way to relate to the musicians who sometimes had the reputation for being a bit temperamental. In fact, choirs are sometimes referred to as the "war department," though I personally never found it so and was blessed by cooperative, helpful musicians.

Even so, one of my favorite questions is simply, "Do you know the difference between a church musician and a terrorist?" The answer, "One can negotiate with a terrorist."

Or, again, a small United Methodist choir would sing, "Will there be any stars, any stars in my crown?" The small Baptist choir across the street would answer, "No, not one; no, not one."

While in college at Emory & Henry, I sang in the quartet and male chorus; and, after I gave up football due to an ankle injury, I joined the band. One time, we were marching in a parade before the Burley Bowl in Johnson City, Tennessee, and a couple of rough-looking fellows pointed to me and yelled, "God, why ain't he playing football?" It was a bit embarrassing, but amusing.

The band provided another amusing incident. Because I had turned my trumpet over to my brother and was playing an E-flat alto horn, I had to transpose the music contemporaneously as I played, and I was making more than my share of bloopers. One day the conductor gave me a particularly severe glare, so I remained after rehearsal to apologize and remind him that I needed proper music. When he apologized, I asked him if he was aware that the French horn player was tone deaf and that not all the horn bloopers were mine. After listening more carefully, the conductor promoted the horn player to majorette. Our conductor gave us some wonderful advice: "If you are going to make a blooper, make one by which to be proud. Gusto is much preferred to hesitancy."

While serving at Munsey Memorial in Johnson City, Tennessee, in the 1980s, we had enough musical talent among our staff to form a quartet. We sang merely for fun but were not bad musically. We tried to come up with a sophisticated name for ourselves. We tried "Staff Inflections," but that sounded too much like staph infections. The congregation settled it for us. We were called "Looney Tunes." It was a real joy, years later, to be part of a reconstituted "Looney Tunes."

In my early days at Munsey, our services were broadcast over the radio. After a few weeks, a member of the congregation timidly asked me to move away from the microphone. Apparently, my loud singing of the bass was confusing the radio audience, and they needed to hear the congregation sing the melody.

Congregations tend to complain that we never sing familiar hymns, so I discovered a way to bridge that chasm by letting everyone submit their favorites. Then, for six months, we only sang those favorites. In a large congregation, that means many hymns are available. When singing someone else's favorite, even an unfamiliar hymn is viewed differently.

I still smile when I remember a district gathering of older adults who were being led by a high-church musician. Someone blurted out, "Why don't we sing some of the old songs?" The director beamed and said, "Thank you, thank you. I, too, love the old hymns. Turn to number so-and-so," a selection which turned out to be a sixth-century Gregorian chant which no one knew. "Old" should be translated as "familiar."

My wife, Carolyn, was a trained, classical musician. She played the piano beautifully and taught private lessons. One of our early churches, Cave Springs, had an all-day singing with a dinner on the grounds. Eleven gospel quartets performed. One of the groups had lost their pianist and asked Carolyn to accompany them. She did such a wonderful job, they tried to sign her up. On the way home, she was quiet and somewhat subdued. I said, "Hon, it was good of you to play, but did you have to play so well that they tried to recruit you?" This had been a cultural shock to say the least. She said quietly, "Don't say another word." And I wisely stayed silent.

Before hymnals were commonly available, a liner would speak the words to be sung. The song leader would then lead the congregation as they sang the words. One evening a famous liner appeared for the service and was invited to line out the hymns. He was not feeling well and meant to decline but instead answered in rhyme: "Mine eyes are dim; I scarce can see to read this hymn at all." The song leader, assuming these words were to a hymn, led the congregation in singing them, to which the liner responded, "I did not mean to sing at all, I think the devil has you all." Again, the congregation sang the spoken words, "I did not mean to sing at all...."

College

College brought another level of fulfillment. I attended Emory & Henry College in Emory, Virginia. Emory & Henry is a small liberal arts Methodist college with a strong faculty and many extracurricular offerings. It was so isolated that the college community became one's family. Our younger son, Jonathan, attended Emory & Henry for one year. He apologized for leaving but said he couldn't go to school in a cow pasture.

In my college days, we would affectionately sing,

Come on down to Emory, boys,
We'll treat you mighty fine,
We'll take all your money and shoot you one big line,
A liberal arts college, eh gads, what a claim.
There's nothing here that's liberal and the arts are all the same.
The girls down here are nutty, the food cannot be found,
But you'll learn to love old Emory if you'll only stick around.

I tested strongly introverted as a 16-year-old freshman and then decidedly extroverted my senior year. There were many opportunities to share in music, drama, athletics, and leadership. Although I was the tallest fellow in our high school, I had not played basketball. However, in college, to help with my football coordination, l was encouraged to try out for the basketball team. I was slow and awkward. The spectators would chant toward the end of the game, "We want Looney! We want Looney!" One time, I was sent in with 50 seconds remaining only to sprain my ankle going for a rebound. The coach was greatly amused to see me dragging off with less than a minute of play.

Our male chorus was student organized and directed. We had a series of exceptional directors. In fact, one student director later led the choral program at Cornell University and another later returned to Emory & Henry as choral director.

One day, we were auditioning for NBC at a Roanoke, Virginia, station. Our 15-minute program had to be perfectly timed. The director gave a cut sign for the chorus to eliminate the next song, but unfortunately, our pianist did not see it. She gave the wrong pitch, which threw the number out of the range of our splendid tenor section. As we reached the big climax of the finale, one of the tenors squatted, turned red in the face, and stuck his fingers in his ears. I had to fight manfully to keep from exploding with laughter.

Our debate team attended a big event in the Northeast, and we were treated to a very formal banquet. One of our team members looked at this stunning array of silverware and proceeded to gather all the excess into a pile so that he was left with only one fork, one knife, and one spoon. His eating experience was simplified, but we were greatly embarrassed.

The president of the college was Dr. Foye Gibson, a former pastor and missionary. He seemed austere, but he had a delicious sense of humor. Someone asked him the difference between being a pastor and a college president. He said he could describe it simply: in the pastorate, he was affectionately known as Brother Foye; at Emory & Henry, he was Brother "Fooey."

On another occasion, Dr. Gibson dismissed a student—a former Marine—for violation of school policies. The student plead earnestly for another chance, but Dr. Gibson assured him that he had no choice. To ease the situation a bit, however, Dr. Gibson informed the student that he planned to be buried on the hill in the Emory & Henry Cemetery and that, after his death, the student could return and spit on his grave. "No, thank you," the student replied. "When I left the Marine Corps, I swore I would never stand in line again for anything."

One of our professors was rumored to grade by the number of pages, not by content. One of our football players—not an outstanding student—decided to test the rumor. At the end of his exam answers, he wrote the Star-Spangled Banner, the Lord's Prayer, and Psalm 23. Sure enough, he received an A. Maybe the professor did stand at the top of the stairs, drop the exam booklets, and give an A to the first ones to land.

One history professor's class inadvertently ended up with only male students. The wife of another professor signed up for the class, but she never attended. Each day for a month, the professor would call her name. It seemed to get funnier by the day. One day, she burst into the classroom and asked innocently, "Am I late?" We roared with laughter, and our professor was completely dumbfounded. She then, just as abruptly as she burst in, left. Someone had apparently informed her of the professor's little game.

Another time, the history professor gave his male students a bit of advice. "One day," he said, "You will meet this dream of your life, the apple of your eye. You will chase her, chase her, and chase her. Then you'll be standing at the altar, and it will hit you like a ton of bricks: I never had a chance."

One Sunday I went with a group of professors to represent the college in local churches. We went individually to churches in one district and then met for lunch. Our music professor ordered his steak well done. When his steak arrived, he cut into it only to have it bleed all over the plate. He motioned to the waiter. "Quick," he said, "Get me a Band-Aid. I believe we can save it."

One of my early roommates had a delicious sense of humor. He was over six feet tall with olive skin and dark, curly hair. He would stand in front of the mirror and say, "I know I'm not good-looking, but what's my opinion against a million women?" As he left the room, he would say, "Ah, you lucky ladies, I'm about to walk across the campus." When a particular character would plop down in our room for an extended visit, he would say, "If you haven't got anything to do, don't do it here," or if that didn't work, he would say, "Make like a tree: leave."

Being geographically isolated, we devised word games to amuse ourselves. Instead of saying, "Twinkle, twinkle, little star," we would recite, "Alternately illuminate, alternately illuminate, infinitesimal asteroid, how I conjugate upon your astronomical location." The phrase "he kicked the bucket" became "he propelled with violence his pedal extremity against the wooden pail which is customarily employed in the transportation of aquatic fluid."

41

We also pondered the omnipotence of God with the question, "Could God make a rock so big he couldn't lift it?" If God could or couldn't, there is limitation. Then we realized that God is limited by choice. God will not do any ungodly thing, nor will God violate our freedom.

After such deep pondering, it was off to seminary at Emory University in Atlanta.

Seminary

Seminary proved to be more of an adventure than anticipated. Alongside the load of classes, I worked in the YMCA Gray Y program coaching football and basketball at an elementary school that was 70% Jewish. In addition, I worked as a youth counselor in one church and later as choir director in another.

Through my work with the YMCA, I volunteered to chaperone 30 thirteen-year-old boys for their patrol leaders' train trip to Washington, D.C. By the time final arrangements had been completed, there were 55 boys. I collected 12 water guns, one hidden in an impressive book that had the middle carved out to conceal the gun. There was little sleep to be had. Before we returned to Atlanta, I had become an overnight prophet breathing fire and brimstone. A free trip had become an unbelievable responsibility.

While in seminary, I also worked at a camp for underprivileged children. Some of the children had never slept on a bed; others had never had a balanced meal. On weekends, we returned to the Wesley House in Atlanta for some R & R. There worked one of the wisest persons I have met, a woman who served us as cook. While many people live beyond their means, she talked about people who lived beneath their privilege. When God has so much to offer, we are so unwilling to receive.

The second year of seminary proved even more dramatic. David Allen and I borrowed enough money to study for a year in Edinburgh, Scotland, at New College where we found James Stewart in New Testament and John Baille in Christian dogmatics to be two of the choice minds and hearts of their generation. Dr. Baille quipped that the Germans create theology, the Americans corrupt theology, and the British correct theology. In addition to our studies, we had a month to bicycle through the British Isles and three months to travel through Europe, staying in youth hostels and meeting students from all over the world.

My size and the antique bicycle I rented created a sensation wherever we went. My bike was made in 1890; four rods from the front and four from the back anchored a seat that was a hammock. It was so high off the ground that my big toe scarcely touched the pavement. My height made this an ideal arrangement, for I was almost standing while seated. Repeated efforts to buy the bicycle failed. Everywhere we went people gathered around to meet the "big Yank" and gawk and gawk at this strange contraption.

The three months on the Continent proved to be equal to another year of study. We visited the great cathedrals, reviewed early Christian history, met the locals, sampled great operas and concerts, struggled with many languages, drank in the beauty of the Alps, to name a few. Equally amazing, I had spent only $1,400 for tuition and lodging, travel and entertainment, and passage by ship to and from the United States.

Easter Vacation
in Great Britain

With an extended break at Easter, David Allen and I began an epic tour of Great Britain on our bicycles. The beautiful scenery of England, Wales, Ireland, Northern Ireland, and Scotland overrode the grueling work of cycling. Nightly stays in youth hostels, populated by students from around the world, expanded our horizons. The charm of quaint villages added flavor to the experience. Extended stays in London and Dublin provided opportunities to visit museums, historic buildings, art galleries, and cathedrals. Performances of opera, ballet, musicals, and orchestras lifted us into a new realm of experience.

While in London, we were able to hear some of the great preachers of the era, such as W.E. Sangster and Leslie Weatherhead, whose writings continue to inspire to this day. A visit to Speakers' Corner in Hyde Park led us to an introduction to Donald Soper, a Methodist preacher and regular presenter there. Each week, he delivered a Christian message and applied it to political and social issues to a varied audience that included atheists, communists, free thinkers, and the like. With his regular attendees, this gathering became like an open-air church and debating society. Over a forty-year ministry, his influence was such that he was knighted by the Queen and became Lord Soper. During an engagement in America, he was asked how he related as a preacher to being called "Lord." His quick, tongue-in-cheek answer was, "I've been reverenced in England for fifty years."

Oxford held special interest for us with its numerous renowned colleges, particularly those associated with the Wesley brothers and the early Methodist movement. Stratford-upon-Avon gave us the opportunity to visit the significant connections of William Shakespeare. The thatched roofs and distinctive buildings were a delight to all photographers of our group. I learned interesting trivia during a visit to Anne Hathaway's cottage. In that time, baths were taken once a year, usually in May. Hence, most weddings were planned in June. Cardiff was the next stop on our way to Ireland. The famous castle was a delight, as was the countryside on the way to the ferry. After settling in Dublin, we enjoyed visits to the university, magnificent churches, and usual sights of interest. As we cycled to Belfast, we were reminded that Ireland is indeed the Emerald Isle. A brief stop in Belfast was followed by a journey along the coast to Carnlough. There the youth hostel was full, so we reluctantly dragged back to the village to search for lodging.

We found an inexpensive inn and went to bed most disappointed. Upon awakening, however, our disappointment soon turned to joy as we discovered our room looked out on an incredible view of the sea, and the food was outstanding. We decided to spend an additional day touring the coast, but the ancient seat on my bicycle fell apart. So, I spent the day weaving a new one with yards of cord as David explored the area. My repaired seat looked a bit pathetic but was adequate for the remainder of our tour.

From Northern Ireland by ferry, we traveled toward the Scottish Highlands. Loch Lomond measured up to all we expected; the hills of Glen Coe were stunning; and the majesty of Ben Nevis stood out, even in the rain and fog. The weather turned so foul that we had to pedal as hard downhill as we did uphill. After three days of continuing wind and rain, the way to Inverness became less and less inviting. From Fort William, the train to Edinburgh delivered two weary travelers to their new home.

Genuine satisfaction and gratitude gripped us as we remembered our month of travel. We had cycled for more than six hundred miles, enjoyed the stunning beauty of five countries, visited with hundreds of foreign students, relished cultural events, and re-lived much of the history learned at home. The "big Yank" had brought many a stare and delighted chuckle from those who observed the ride on that 1890 bicycle. I rode it for the next five weeks for day trips from Edinburgh and then returned it reluctantly upon departure.

Hitchhiking
Through Europe

At end of our studies in Edinburgh, with three months remaining before the fall term at Emory University, we embarked on a grand tour of Europe. Hitchhiking was to be our preferred method of transportation. By the end of summer, we had covered seven thousand miles by thumb, foot, and public transport. Again, youth hostels provided inexpensive lodging and numerous opportunities to converse with students from across the globe. These exchanges and the varied cultures of Europe gave us an expanded view of the world and our place in it.

From Edinburgh, we headed north to Inverness, Scotland. The scenery through the highlands of Scotland and Lake District of England added to our storehouse of favorite memories. We attended an awe-inspiring worship service at Canterbury Cathedral in which six priests were ordained by the archbishop.

The pomp and solemnity of the service made a profound impression.

Upon crossing the English Channel from Dover, the journey through Europe began. Even without the ancient bike, we continued to be the object of curiosity. The large backpacks contained clothes for the summer, suit and ties for concerts, reading material for rainy days, a tent, sleeping bags, maps, and cooking utensils. A forty-pound backpack helped develop strength and endurance seldom imagined. Some days our walking time exceeded riding time, and other days included several hours of impatient waiting. We visited France, Switzerland, Italy, Austria, Germany, Brussels, the Netherlands, Denmark, Sweden, Norway, and Scotland.

Highlights of the trip included lengthy stays in Paris and Rome, extended travel through the Alps, shopping for food in a strange language, visiting with new friends through grunts and smiles, attempting to sleep in noisy hostel dorms, developing patience as hundreds of cars sped by, and surviving unpleasant weather. The astounding, however, outweighed the difficult by large measure.

Paris readily deserves its reputation as one of the world's most beautiful cities; the Alps defy description, leaving a sense of profound awe; and

Rome, with the Vatican, illumine so much of the early days of Christianity. In the catacombs, one remembers the persecution that drove the Christians underground. The splendor of the Roman Empire, seen in its surviving buildings, illustrates the unlikely survival of the movement that would spread around the world.

Through this summer of travel, we experienced the wonder of creation; the presence of God in worship, even in unfamiliar languages; and kinship with God's children from all cultures and races. My own heart was enlarged immeasurably and my education greatly enhanced. Growing up on a mountain farm and in a small mining town, I could never have imagined that there was such a world to be explored.

Back Home

Once back in Atlanta, the third year of seminary was even more life-changing. I returned to a heavy load of classes and my YMCA and church work. But, in one of my classes was a dark-haired beauty from Mississippi named Carolyn. She caught my eye and captured my heart, and in a few months, we were engaged. I was amazed by how much we had in common and how easily we shared our deepest thoughts. She was the ideal companion for the journey ahead and the perfect wife for a preacher.

Our meeting had its own humor. Having spent two terms in Scotland, I had lost some credit hours. To catch up, I needed to take 18 hours each quarter. In this first quarter, the only extra class I could schedule was called *Church and Recreation,* a two-hour class that met on Monday evening. Carolyn, who was majoring in Christian education, was required to take that particular class.

Our professor talked about many activities, including folk games. As the class ended, he said we would play games outside some evening in the moonlight. As we left the building, a full moon lit the campus. My roommate and I were first behind Carolyn and her roommate. Carolyn turned and said, "Would you like to play games in the moonlight?" I answered, "That sounds like a great idea." I enjoyed retelling about this moonlight invitation, even though Carolyn insisted that she thought the whole class was behind them.

Anyway, I was smitten by Carolyn's beauty immediately upon observing this special lady in the class. Our courtship survived the first date when I foolishly asked her to go with me as I led a youth group to a skating party. I could not skate, and Carolyn inherited the chore of teaching me. At the end of the evening, the owner of the skating rink presented her with a medal for valor.

In the midst of the drama, there was a lot of fun to be remembered and enjoyed. Some of the professors were filled with humor as well as devotion. Dr. Stokes—later Bishop—loved to talk about preachers and teachers who ought to be arrested for indecent mental exposure.

Dean Cannon—later Bishop—had a brilliant mind but provided many illustrations of the absentminded professor. For instance, having forgotten that he drove downtown one day, he was reported to have returned home by bus. Another time, he asked his friend, Dr. Stokes, to buy him a new car. When asked what kind, he replied, "Blue." He once left a date abruptly, and when he didn't return, she went outside the theatre to find him sitting under a lamp writing furiously. A sudden inspiration caused him to forget his date and the occasion.

Our homiletics professor could be funny, even in his hard-hitting critiques of our sermons delivered in class. He was particularly rough on a student pastor who finally replied, "I don't understand. I preached this sermon Sunday, and four people were moved to tears." The professor replied, "I can understand perfectly. It's all I can do to keep from crying myself."

Another student preached on the miraculous catch of fish after Jesus instructed the disciples to pitch their net on the other side of the boat. When the student referred to the "fruit of their labor," the professor sprang to his feet shouting, "Fruit?!? Fruit?!? What did they catch? Apples? Oranges? Bananas? Fruit? Fruit? They caught FISH! FISH!"

The homiletics professor could be quite dramatic in his class lectures as well. One day he was lecturing away when he suddenly crouched right in front of me and shouted, "Why?" His question made no sense. I wanted to shout, "Why what? What are you talking about?" Instead, I just stared at him as he stared at me. Then he stepped back and shouted, "Have you come out of your coma yet?" The class roared.

Someone started the habit of saying, "Boy, that'll preach." It was particularly used when something trite or inane had been said. One of my friends, who had a loud voice, was particularly fond of saying it sarcastically. One day a visiting professor was diagramming Einstein's theory of relativity on the chalkboard. No one had a clue about how this applied to preaching. Suddenly, from the back of the room, a loud voice spoke out, "Boy, that'll preach." The professor quietly turned and said, "Gentlemen, we have witnessed an Old Testament miracle: Balaam's ass has just spoken." You can imagine the roar of laughter—and the number of times we brayed when we saw our friend.

Another professor liked to begin his classes with poetry. One day he dramatically began, "I saw God in a tree." From the back of the room came a voice heard by the class but not the professor: "That wasn't God; that was a squirrel." The professor never knew the cause of all the laughter.

Two of my seminary friends were gifted preachers and often shared in preaching revivals. One was preaching one night and spoke of "Moses in the lions' den." His buddy softly whispered, "Daniel," but Moses kept being referenced. As the whisperer grew louder, the one preaching finally stopped and said, "Oh, yes, it was Daniel, wasn't it?" and kept preaching without missing a beat. Later, his friend was assigned to the Nolichucky Circuit near Johnson City, Tennessee. He was a passionate preacher who put his whole being into preparing and preaching. After his first six months, someone asked an older woman how she liked her new preacher. "Oh," she said, "we love him to death." Then pausing, she said, "But to tell you the truth, I'm just worn out by being converted every Sunday."

From Seminary
to the Pastorate

Since I had grown up in the home of a Methodist preacher, I had a general idea of what was expected of a pastor. My first appointment was to the three-point circuit in Rising Fawn, Georgia (Byrd's Chapel, Cave Springs, and Rising Fawn), a part of the Holston Conference. In Hillsville, Virginia, the place of my birth, my dad had served a four-point circuit. As young preachers, we loved to say if you had five talents, they gave you five churches; if you had three talents, three churches; one talent, one church; and if you had no talents, you were appointed a district superintendent or elected as bishop. After I became each one of these, the humor had a different tone but was still enjoyable.

I already knew that preaching was very important and that pastoral care was most crucial, but I soon learned that administration and stewardship cultivation were also essential.

With three churches, I preached three times on Sunday and visited parishioners regularly during the week. Between the three churches, there were about 160 members, and I could easily visit each family monthly. I also prepared a monthly newsletter and performed other office duties. The mornings were given to study and sermon preparation.

The people received Carolyn and me most graciously, and I was feeling quite satisfied with my performance. After about six months, the "Colonel" brought me back to earth. He said, "We are sick and tired of training all these greenhorn preachers. About the time they know what they are doing, they are moved off and we get another greenhorn." As it so happened, they had received a series of seminary graduates and were ready for someone with experience. I am sure there will be a special place in heaven for small churches that loved and encouraged greenhorn preachers like myself.

Later, Colonel, who often spoke abruptly, did us all a great favor. At the time, the district offered stewardship training for pastors and lay leaders in which we were taught to set a dream budget, asking what we would like to do if money were no object. Alongside that, we were to calculate the giving potential of the congregation: "What could we give if we gave like a Christian steward?"

The dream budget came in at 150% of the current one, a 50% increase. The potential stewardship budget came in at double the current level, a 100% increase. In the inspiration of the moment, the Colonel moved that we adopt the entire dream budget, a 50% increase, and the official board voted unanimously to do so. Only later did we question the foolish thing we had done. To our amazement, however, the budget was met, and finances were no longer an issue!

During this time, I heard of another inspirational stewardship story. A small church was in such bad straits financially that they owed every business in town and couldn't pay their bills. In addition, the treasurer had resigned. The town miller, to whom the people brought their grain to be ground, finally agreed to serve if they wouldn't ask for a financial report for a year. At the end of the year, the church members eagerly awaited the treasurer's report.

"You remember that when I took this job, we owed every business in town?" he asked.

"Oh, yes," they replied.

"Well, all our bills are current," he reported.

"Wonderful, wonderful," they said.

"You also remember that we owed $25,000 on our building?" he added.

"Oh, yes, we won't be able to pay that off for twenty years," they confessed.

"Well, it's paid off," he assured them.

"No way," they murmured. "Stop kidding us."

"Oh, yes," he answered, "and now we have $25,000 in the bank."

"You are really putting us on now. How is this possible?" they shouted.

"Well," he said, "Remember, I'm the miller. When you brought me your grain, I just took out the Lord's portion, the tithe. You didn't miss it, and we've paid all our bills, retired our debt, and have money in the bank."

What pastor wouldn't covet such a treasurer?

Thankfully, the opportunity to share in the lives of different people continued in the pastoral ministry. Small-membership churches with limited resources have found ways to raise funds to meet human need. In my first appointment, one of the churches raised cotton to supplement its budget. My wife, a city girl, wore blisters with a hoe handle and learned to quilt. I learned to smooth concrete when we added a four-room addition to the sanctuary.

In our second appointment, Pleasant View UMC, we learned to plant, harvest, and grade peppers. After two years of selling peppers for $50 and $55 a ton, we concluded that there must be a better way to supplement the budget. One man decided to give a pig from a litter as part of a Lord's Acre project. He selected the runt of the litter but later reported that this pig outgrew all the others. God apparently had the last laugh.

There seems to be a real connection between generous giving and strong faith. Maybe as we trust God with our means, we come to see that we can trust God with our time and talents, even ourselves as well. Yet people still become sensitive when money is mentioned in church. One woman sent word that she was not coming back to church because all we talked about was money. Sure enough, she had attended church twice that year, and as luck would have it, I had preached on stewardship those two Sundays.

Sometimes people say they want a spiritual preacher who doesn't talk about material things. Little do they realize that such a definition would leave Jesus out as well. His teachings are full of references regarding use of our material possessions. In fact, some of the deepest spiritual growth in churches I have served has come because of second-mile giving for a building or mission project.

Visiting—though necessary, I assumed—was not always easy. I had become more outgoing through college and seminary, but I was still timid. I was not always sure how to carry on a meaningful conversation, and truthfully, sometimes I was relieved when no one answered the door.

One of my friends, who was even more timid, was visiting one day. Someone else dropped in and found my friend reading the paper while the woman was reading her mail. Neither of them knew how to keep a conversation going.

Knowing how to conduct an evangelistic visit was particularly difficult for me, and when it came to pressing someone to make a Christian commitment, I was especially ill at ease. Slowly, I came to realize that God was working in people's lives, and the whole responsibility was not mine to bear. One time, I worked for a week trying to plan the best approach to use with a young man who was attending church but was not a professing Christian. I even had a speech worked out for "converting him." When he opened the door, he said, "Thank God, I wanted to talk to you about being a Christian." I stammered a bit, realizing that my eloquent speech was unnecessary. I just needed to show up.

Early in my ministry, I wrote a special sermon for a young man who was an outstanding athlete and highly respected mason. In the sermon, I compared the Christian faith to an athletic contest. When I gave an invitation to Christian discipleship, he came forward to make a profession of faith. I beamed with pride, and the congregation was overjoyed. But when I visited him later, the young man revealed he had not heard the sermon at all. The night before, I had used an illustration about faith from Billy Graham, and it had haunted him for twenty-four hours. He came to church that evening determined to become a follower and simply awaited the invitation to do so. God works in mysterious ways his wonders to perform.

On another occasion, I gave a routine invitation at the end of my sermon. A young woman burst from her pew, came to the front, knelt at the altar, and made a Christian commitment. During a home visit that week, I asked her, "What was it I said in the sermon that moved you?" She smiled and admitted, "I didn't hear a word you said. God has been working in my life, and I came to church to make my decision. I was just praying for a brief sermon so I could do what I had planned."

Most of us struggle with how to share our faith and can relate to the story of a country boy who wanted to share his faith. The boy went out to a very rural area, saw a man sitting on the porch in a rocking chair. He stopped and asked the man, "Are you a Christian?"

"No," said the man. "I'm a Smith. The Christians live up the road about a half mile on the left."

The young man tried again: "I mean are you lost?"

"No," replied the fellow. "I've lived here all my life. I know right where I am."

Again, the young man tried: "Are you ready for the judgment day?"

The fellow replied, "When is it?"

"I don't know," the young man said. "It may be today, it may be tomorrow," to which the fellow begged, "Don't tell my wife. She'll want to go both days."

Not everyone welcomes the preacher's visit. People are so busy that one hesitates to impose on their time. Sometimes your knock is ignored. I would love to have seen the position some folks "froze" in when they heard the knock. They were noisily stirring about until the knock on the door; then, utter and complete silence. One memorable day, I left home with a list of seven shut-ins to visit. Not one of them was in. Some are apparently infirm only on Sunday. One woman who was too ill to attend church was observed for three hours at a football game on a windy night running all about the bleachers.

Yet, I continued to visit. I visited one family repeatedly to encourage their attendance at church. It was time to visit them again, but I was fed up. Again and again, they had promised to attend but didn't. I almost drove away, but out of habit, I turned into their drive. When the woman saw me at the door, she said, "I don't know why you keep coming by, we never keep our promises." Instead of saying, "I don't know either," I just smiled.

The next Sunday, the family came. They did not miss a Sunday for my last two years there and became leaders in the church. God may not need our eloquence or clever arguments, but somehow God honors our efforts for showing up.

Athletics provided another way to relate to people where we lived. One church had a bowling team; another, softball, and basketball teams. As part of the team, parishioners could relate to me as a human being as well as a pastor. When age ended my playing days, I became a vocal fan and supporter. In fact, my wife had to remind me frequently that I was called to preach, not instruct the officials.

Preaching also presents some interesting challenges—such as distractions and time—but there is probably no more challenging task than to properly interpret the scriptures and apply them to daily living. Admittedly, it can be tempting to misuse the text for one's own purposes. For instance, when women started wearing a hairstyle called "top knot," an old preacher was sure God was not pleased. So, he searched the scriptures and found the proper text "top (k)not come down." In the text, Jesus was warning about the end of time when he said, "Those on the housetop not come down." By ignoring the context, the preacher created his own misleading text.

One of my friends was serving a church near Atlanta. On a Sunday when he was not well prepared, a Candler School of Theology professor dropped in to the service. Realizing that the professor might return, he prepared well for the next Sunday. Referring to the prior week's feeble effort, my friend said to the professor, "I hope I didn't misuse the text." "No," said the professor, "You didn't even use it."

Even when well prepared, distractions can be devastating. In one of my small churches, there were three adorable babies. During the service, these babies were passed around the congregation lovingly. On occasion, I was tempted to say, "Hello! Anyone listening? The name's Looney. I'm preaching. Is anyone listening?"

Then there are distractions like howling dogs under the back pew; swarms of wasps around the pulpit; giggling, whispering teenagers in the balcony; the sleeping saints; and on and on. One writer wrote a stirring essay describing the sermon as a work of art. My friend wrote a reply saying he had probably never preached in the country with crying babies and howling dogs; there the sermon was an act of survival.

In an age of TV and video games, it becomes increasingly important for the sermon to be concise and to the point. My mother had a saying about long sermons: "He ran by a half-dozen good stopping places." I made the mistake of sharing that comment with my wife, Carolyn, and she said it a few times after hearing me go on and on.

My dad was a strong preacher and easily held the congregation's attention for thirty minutes. One night while preaching in a revival, he put his watch down on the pulpit during the hymn preceding the sermon. As the hymn was finished, he inadvertently placed the hymnal on top of the watch. As Dad preached, he began to search for his watch, going through his pockets repeatedly. His usual thirty-minute sermon stretched to forty, fifty, and then sixty minutes. After the service, he rushed to the back to greet people. As he passed me, he whispered, "Did I quit too soon?" If I had not been so tired after sixty minutes, I would have laughed.

When I was assigned to Munsey Memorial in Johnson City, Tennessee, I found a magnificent sanctuary with a high, impressive pulpit. Above the pulpit was an ornate sounding board. One man gave me some friendly advice: "People will tell you that above your head is a sounding board, but it's really a preacher snuffer. It lowers precisely at 12 o'clock, and you had best be out of the pulpit."

In a roast of a fellow preacher, one man described preaching as drilling for oil. "But my friend," he said, "could drill deeper, go longer, and come up drier than anyone he knew."

Mission Trips

A team of people from Holston Conference went to Liberia, West Africa, to teach and preach for several weeks. On our last Sunday, we were assigned to preach in several churches out from Monrovia. One of our preachers had a bee-sting kit, lest his next sting be fatal. In the excitement of the morning, he forgot his kit. As he mounted the high English-style pulpit, wasps were flying about in great numbers. The congregation was singing "Nearer, My God, to Thee." Ben reported that never had a hymn seemed so appropriate.

My first mission trip was to Peru. A team from Holston Conference did construction work and conducted evening services. The Peruvians, who typically are short in stature, called me "El Grand Hombre."

For the first time—and with mixed results—I preached through an interpreter. After doing so, I heard an amusing story of an American preacher in Latin America. The preacher would speak in short sentences for thirty seconds, and then his interpreter would translate for two minutes. Frustrated, the preacher asked the translator if he was telling the people what he was saying. "Oh, no," was the reply. "I am improving on it greatly."

I also participated in a mission trip to Belize where teams from South Georgia built a church building in a poverty-stricken area. As a courtesy to our team, the local people invited me to preach the opening sermon. The prime minister, who was a devout Roman Catholic, attended the service. As we were introduced, he kissed my ring and called me "my Lord." Upon returning home, I shared the story with my district superintendents and said more respect should now be shown to "my Lord." They said if they had been there, they would have said, "Have Mercy."

Pulpit Exchanges

The World Methodist Council promotes and arranges pulpit exchanges for Methodist pastors throughout the world. In this program, pastors and their families move into the other family's home, use their vehicle, and serve their churches for approximately six weeks. We were fortunate to participate in two such exchanges.

Our first assignment was to Keswick, England, in the beautiful Lake District. The scenery was as close to heaven as imaginable. The English may be known for keeping a stiff upper lip, but we found them amazingly warm and welcoming. Incidentally, the English pastor drove a Mini car into which crammed five large Looneys. People came early to church and stayed late to observe this strange and comical sight. Our family even managed to accomplish days of sightseeing without incident in that Mini.

Keswick was one of ten churches on a large circuit
served by retired and lay pastors and the senior
minister. With this arrangement, we visited several
congregations, including Cockermouth where
Wordsworth attended school. The Fourth of July
occurred during our visit, so the people were eager
to honor us with an American celebration. They
apparently talked to someone who confused American
traditions, for we had a wonderful turkey-and-dressing
spread. We were so grateful for their thoughtfulness
that we never mentioned hotdogs or hamburgers.
Many invitations were extended to come for tea or
high tea. This delightful tradition filled our stomachs
and warmed our hearts. We made delightful friends
and exchanged future visits. One of the retired pastors
there allowed us to view a bucket of Roman coins found
in his yard.

During our exchange, the town hosted the
famous Keswick Convention, a gathering of
evangelical Christians from many countries and
traditions. All shared in the services and in Holy
Communion, reminding us that we are truly one
in Christ. Billy Graham addressed a gathering of
several hundred pastors, and I was privileged to greet
him personally. Each day, the Methodist Church
hosted participants for tea and all the goodies that went
with it, and on Sunday evenings, the church presented

a slide show of the Lake District. The beauty of creation provided another kind of worship experience.

Our two teenagers and eight-year-old benefited greatly from this experience. On the return home, we enjoyed three days each in London and Paris.

The second exchange was in Parramatta, Australia, and did not include the children. The church of 400 members was in a suburb of Sydney. They had an incredible number of ministries with people on the edges of society: a home for homeless men that could care for sixty, a hostel for working young adults, a farm for youth at risk. In Australia, the government will fund social programs through local churches where they are managed with less waste.

Between Sundays, we were able to visit other major cities: the Blue Mountains, the Gold Coast, and Sydney. The harbor and opera building were breathtaking, and the Australian people were very warm, welcoming, and fun-loving. We also visited with the Alan Walkers, world-renowned Methodists. Again, we were privileged to experience the expanse of the Christian movement that embraces the world and its people.

Other High Holy Moments

In addition to the wonder of preaching, visiting, and leading a congregation, the pastor is privileged to be God's representative in some of people's most sacred moments. Who is adequate for such a responsibility and privilege? Some have said the pastor is present for the hatching (birth), matching (wedding), and dispatching (death), but even funny things happen in these inspiring moments. For instance, a distinguished pastor was baptizing a mountain family, but a young boy was resisting the occasion, hiding behind his mother's skirt. Finally, the pastor took water from the baptismal font and flicked it on the youngster, who then brought the house down when he shouted, "That SOB threw water on me!"

Another young boy was crying on the way home from church after his infant brother had been baptized. They were puzzled that he was weeping after such an inspiring service. When asked what the matter was, he responded, "The preacher prayed that we would grow up in a Christian home, but I want to stay with you guys."

During a children's sermon, another preacher was going to talk about God being everywhere. He asked, "Do you know where God is?" A little boy's hand shot up. "I know," he said. The preacher then asked, "Where is God?" "In the bathroom," the boy said with assurance. When asked why he said that, he answered, "Every morning my daddy stands at the bathroom door and shouts, 'My God, are you still in there?'"

During one children's sermon, I was telling a dramatic story about the time our son was lost and we had the whole community helping us search for him. A little girl spoke up loudly, "That's a made-up story, isn't it?" I laughed along with everyone else.

When I was in seminary, Dad wrote to inquire about my next trip home: he had a 300-pound man who wished to be baptized in the river by immersion, and he would need help to lift him up from the water.

In Cave Springs, my first appointment, a young man wished to be baptized by immersion. Several Baptists attended the service out of curiosity, thinking that Methodists only baptized by sprinkling. They would ask, "Are you going to be baptized or sprinkled?" My efforts to teach them to say, "Are you going to be baptized by immersion or by sprinkling" gained little headway, nor did I succeed in explaining that ships are christened; babies are baptized.

Weddings also provide lighter moments. When I arrived at Munsey Memorial in 1979, they were still talking about the wedding a few months earlier. When asked, "Who giveth this woman to be married to this man?" the father replied, "The Johnson City banks, her mother, and I."

Having given a daughter in marriage, I especially appreciate the story of the man who asked his friend what it was like to give a daughter away. His friend said, "Imagine that you have a priceless Stradivarius violin. It's fragile, delicate, irreplaceable. You walk it lovingly and carefully down this long aisle and then place it in the hands of a gorilla." Someone added that it's amazing that the most undeserving and inadequate son-in-law can be the father of perfect grandchildren.

When one of my college friends was married, his fraternity brothers kidnapped his bride before the reception and brought her back to the church after thirty minutes. The groom, however, had been so busy visiting with guests that he had not even missed her— not the best way to begin married life.

My dad's first appointment was to the Hillsville, Virginia, circuit. Virginia did not have a waiting period after obtaining a marriage license, and as a result, many couples came over from North Carolina to get married. On one Saturday alone, Dad performed sixteen weddings. When asked by one of the grooms, "How much do I owe you?" he would mischievously say, "Whatever the bride is worth." One fellow replied to Dad's quip with his own humor: "I ain't got no pennies." The bride was not greatly amused.

My first appointment at Rising Fawn, Georgia, in Dade County, had no waiting period either, so dozens of folks came from Alabama for a quick wedding. On one occasion, I was trying to counsel a couple before the ceremony. I was not yet married and knew not of which I spoke, and the session was not going well. Finally, the groom said, "Ah, Preacher, let's get on with it." I was as relieved as he was to "get on with it."

A judge who lived in Rising Fawn was known far and wide as "the marrying judge." If he came out to the car, the charge was five dollars; if the ceremony took place on his porch, ten dollars; but, in his living room on his oriental rug, the cost jumped to twenty-five dollars.

Occasionally something funny happens at a funeral. In my first appointment, another Methodist pastor and I were sharing in a funeral where both of us were to speak and lead prayers. We closed the service, sat down, and waited for the funeral director. After some time, someone went looking for him. With two preachers to speak, he assumed he had at least an hour to kill and had gone for a walk.

Sometimes preachers seem to outdo themselves in talking about how close they were to the deceased or in extolling the virtues of the departed. The widow of one such character whispered to her son to slip out and peek in the casket; she did not recognize the person being described so glowingly.

One of the inspiring moments in a military service is the firing of the rifles. At one such service, the shock of the unexpected firing of the guns caused the grandmother to keel over in a faint. One of the grandchildren cried, "Good Lord, they shot Grandma."

In South Georgia, they tell about the death of the town's worst character. No one could think of anything good to say about him, but they felt that he deserved something kind. Then they remembered an old gentleman who was always able to say something good about everyone, and they asked him to give the eulogy. He did his best: "Everyone knows," he said, "that old Joe was not always as bad as he was most of the time."

Sometimes preachers are asked to conduct a service for a beloved animal. A Methodist pastor was asked to do such a service for a special dog. At first, the pastor announced that he could not do that, but he would find a

Baptist preacher who would. The owner inquired if a $500 honorarium would be sufficient for the preacher. Suddenly, the preacher had a change of heart. "I didn't realize that we were talking about a Methodist dog," he said.

Preachers' Kids

Being the child of a preacher, I became aware that PKs had the reputation of being unruly or over-the-top. My dad informed his congregations that there was an obvious explanation for this: we had to play with their children. He added that we were expected to act as normal children, even taking on bullies when necessary.

My brother, David, was easygoing until provoked beyond his limit. Once the town bully pushed David too far and fled to his home when confronted. In a rage, David followed him inside and dragged him out for a good whipping. The boy's mother had a reputation for protecting her son through every circumstance. With that fact in mind, David was very late in arriving home the following afternoon. To avoid going near the feared mother's home, he had taken the long way home around a nearby mountain.

That brings to mind the experiences of our three children: Teresa, David, and Jonathan. Those of you who are parents are aware of the uniqueness of each child. How could they be so different with the same parents and home influences?

Teresa was our firstborn and demonstrated a strong will early on. When her mother laid out her clothes for kindergarten, she would ignore them and proceed to select her own from the dresser. Teresa did not appreciate the congregation expecting more from her than they did from their children. A poster from her early teens expressed clear self-assurance. Under the picture of a regal cat were the words, "Everyone is entitled to my opinion."

David was quieter but strong-willed, nevertheless. On one occasion, he became engrossed in watching some bantam chickens his grandfather had brought by. Incidentally, the district superintendent had joined the crowd. In a bit of fun, the superintendent poked David in the ribs. That jab startled him so that David spun and hit him with his fist. A forgiving man enjoyed the outburst.

At the age of four, David asked the ultimate theological question, "Where did babies come from when everyone was a baby?" I wisely told him to ask his mother. At about the same age, he became fascinated by the fact that Carolyn was four years older than me. Whenever we had company, he would soon announce, "You know what? My mother is four years older than my daddy!" Carolyn became resigned to these frequent announcements.

Our third child, Jonathan, arrived six years after the birth of David and profited from all we had learned from the first two. For several years, he spent worship time in the church nursery. When it was time to graduate from the nursery, Carolyn brought him with her to the Sunday evening hour. This informal service was led by a lay person, so I was not seen until time for the sermon. When I arose to preach, this boy, who had been amazingly quiet, yelled, "That's my Daddy!" For that evening, he returned to the nursery.

Frequent moves are difficult for children as their schools, churches, and friendships are disrupted. Breaking into new circles is challenging. We were moved just before Teresa's senior year but arranged a 30-mile commute for her and frequent overnights with friends. David felt cheated but would have faced three years of commuting, and Jonathan was expected to move with us at twelve years of age. Jonathan came out of a "blue funk" when he learned that Johnson City had cable TV.

To my children's credit, they managed the difficult

adjustments and made special friends wherever we lived.

Preacher Stories

The following are some of my favorite preacher stories. Lee Hill and I served together in Dade County, Georgia. Lee was quiet but had a delicious sense of humor. At his retirement recognition, he recounted his first days of ministry. He was living at the Children's Home in Greeneville and seeking an appointment, partially to escape the cornfield at the home. The week before conference, the superintendent called to say it looked as if no appointment would be available. In his disappointment, he prayed deeply and earnestly. But, Lee said, he must have over-prayed, for a week later, the superintendent called to say they had a charge with ten churches for him to serve.

I had been asked to lead the singing for a revival in Lee's county-seat church. One evening, there was a special sense of the Lord's presence during the sermon. Lee announced that instead of a public invitation, he wanted everyone to pray quietly. He asked the pianist, who was the mayor's wife, to play hymn number 121, "Silently." This proper lady opened her book, lifted her hands, and thought silently. She lowered her hands, and in a moment, lifted them again silently. Again she lowered her hands. The third time she lifted her hands, she thought maybe he meant "softly." The inspiration of the moment left me as I stifled a laugh.

One of my older friends was Joe Hampton. He was a strong preacher and a noted singer. His bishop described him as "a preacher of note and a singer at the slightest provocation." I was to preach a revival at St. Elmo United Methodist Church in Chattanooga where Joe attended in his retirement. He was not there that Sunday morning, as he was away preaching for a sick pastor. That evening I told him I had missed him, and he reported on his morning sermon. Joe was 75 at the time and full of vitality. He told me that he had preached with his usual vim and vigor and then sang a solo. At the end of the service, a gentleman came out, shaky and using a cane. "Oh, Brother, it's so good to see you young fellows with so much vim and vigor. I'm so old and feeble." "How old are you, brother?" asked Brother Hampton. With trembling voice, he answered, "I'm going on 61." Brother Joe reminded me again he was 75.

Another older minister, Cato Dick, was a great

encourager. Originally from Norway, he came to Boston University to study for the ministry. To meet expenses, he served a small church in the area. On one occasion, he called the leader of the Women's Society to set up a meeting. She informed him that she was tied up every Tuesday and Thursday but could meet him any other time. Not understanding American slang, he wondered what kind of strange marital arrangement she and her husband had.

Even the practice of individual prayer presents moments of levity. One man went on a long-needed diet. His coworkers noted how diligent he had become. The man even changed his route to work to avoid the local bakery. But, after several weeks of real discipline, he arrived with a calorie-laden coffee cake. The coworkers immediately asked what happened. For some reason, he had returned to the old route, and there was this tempting cake in the window. So, he prayed, "Lord, if you want me to have that cake, provide me a parking place right in front of the front door." And God did just that. On the eighth turn around the block, there was a spot in front.

Once during a conference at Lake Junaluska, several young preachers were eating at Granny's Chicken Palace just off the grounds. We were having a hilarious time. It is easy to let one's hair down with peers as pressures of the church are shared. We must have really loosened up for someone overheard our waitress say, "Do you see that table over there? They are so drunk they think they are Methodist preachers."

An old evangelist that helped my dad in several revivals had a fascinating way of expressing himself. He talked about people who had "buzzard" religion: they only showed up at church when someone died. He called "smoking" "burning incense to the devil." He was suspicious of women's makeup. Lipstick was called "lipping stick." He was full of stories about farm meals. In one story, a large hog was chased from the kitchen with a whack on the back from a gravy ladle. The hog ran under the preacher's stool and carried him right out into the yard.

My dad could be very straightforward when needed but amazingly sensitive at other times. Someone had invited a Gospel quartet to sing in one of the revival services where Dad was preaching, and they were unusually bad—embarrassingly so. When Dad followed their discordant music, he smiled and said, "Folks, don't we appreciate the effort of these men?" They beamed with appreciation.

One of the strong leaders of Holston Conference was serving at Brainerd UMC in Chattanooga. One Tuesday, he looked at his calendar and realized that he was supposed to have had lunch with a member of his congregation at her home on Monday. He was mortified. He called immediately to apologize, saying how embarrassed he was, explaining he just did not understand how that could have happened. There was a long silence before she said, "Brother Tom, you were here."

One Sunday, a young preacher preached unusually well, and the people responded enthusiastically. On the way home, he asked his wife how many great preachers there were now in America. She replied, "I don't know, honey, but there's one less than you think." We all need someone to bring us back to Earth on occasion and, on other occasions, to lift us up.

All of us have had an embarrassing slip of the tongue. One of my friends had invited my father to help him in a series of revival services. At that time, it was customary to spend the afternoon making visits in the parish. At the close of a visit with Brother Helmendollar, the pastor prayed that God would bless Brother "Humdinger."

Most of these stories happened, but some are too good to be true. A pastor and his wife were inseparable, but after 25 years of closeness, she was called away for two weeks to deal with a family emergency. Before leaving, she cooked and froze a wonderful variety of food for his enjoyment. Just as they were parting, she said, "Oh, by the way, there's a box under our bed that is like a personal diary. You are not to look in it." He replied that he would not think of such a thing.

But after the fourth day, experiencing acute loneliness, he decided to take a look, sure that she would understand. In the box, the pastor found three eggs and $10,000. He thought that was strange, but he replaced the box so his wife would never know. At the end of two weeks, she returned for an affectionate reunion. All was well until his conscience began to bother him. So, about midnight, he awakened her to confess his violation of trust. "You what?" she said. "You looked in the box? I can't believe you violated my trust." "I know, honey. That was terrible, but I knew you would forgive me. We did marry for better or worse, after all."

Finally, she offered forgiveness, and they settled back for sleep. But he couldn't leave well enough alone. So, at 2:00 a.m., he awakened her again. "I'm sorry, honey. Tell me about the three eggs and $10,000." She said, "When we married, I told God that I would put an egg in the box every time you preached a really bad sermon." "Well," he thought. "That's not bad, 25 years, two sermons every Sunday, and only three eggs." Then he made a serious error. "How about the $10,000?" "Oh," she replied. "Every time I got a dozen, I sold them."

Some preachers have a reputation for fast driving, the heavy foot. One such preacher hit a mountain curve too fast, slid off the road, and rolled down the hillside. Another motorist, heavily under the influence, stopped to help. He called out, "Preacher, are you okay?" The preacher announced that he was fine, for the Lord was with him, to which his impaired friend responded, "You better let the Lord ride with me. You are going to kill him the way you are driving."

Out of courtesy to a church member, I attended the funeral in which a pastor preached a 45-minute sermon, then called the widow to come forward and repent of her sins so she would not burn in hell with her husband. Later, the pastor—who distrusted fancy education, especially that found in seminaries— prayed for the Lord to make him more ignorant. A lay person who heard that request commented, "Not even God could answer that prayer!"

A young seminary student returned to Chattanooga to preach in his home church on a particular Sunday. Everyone told him how great he was and how proud they were of him. Feeling quite proud of himself, he went over to an older preacher who happened in that morning to ask what he thought of the sermon. To his regret, the old preacher told him exactly what he thought: "First, you read it; second, you don't read very well, and third, it was not worth reading."

A Dade County preacher, who lived on Sand Mountain and worked in Chattanooga during the week, bought a new Volkswagen Beetle to drive for his commute. Each weekday, unbeknownst to the preacher, one of his members added a gallon of fuel to his tank. On Sunday morning, some of the men gathered after the service to quiz him about the new car—especially about the gas mileage—but the preacher refused to answer. After much urging, the preacher said, "You will accuse me of lying." "No, no," they said. "Well," he said hesitantly, "I am getting one hundred miles to the gallon!" They then let him in on their scheme.

I have owned and driven several Volkswagens, including two Beetles. With plenty of leg and head room, they were surprisingly roomy for a big man. So, I have always enjoyed Beetle stories. One such story described a man who was hit by a Beetle and then sent to the hospital to have it removed. Another involved a woman who bought a Beetle. Later, she decided to check the engine, so she lifted the front hood, and then called the police to report the engine stolen. When the police arrived, they opened the back to show her the intact engine. "How cute," she said, "It has a spare."

In the early 1960s, a preaching mission was held in

the East Tennessee area, and some of the outstanding preachers of America were invited. As organized, services were held in four area cities. In each of those services, local pastors sat on the stage and participated in the order of service. The pastor who was to introduce a distinguished preacher from New York City was himself presented as the pastor of the First Christian Church. Coming forward, the man heatedly responded that he was not the pastor of the Christian Church but the Baptist Church. The brusque manner of his response created a tense moment. The guest, in an effort to lighten the moment said, "It was worth my long trip to the Tri-Cities this year to hear a Baptist admit that he was not a Christian." The rolling laughter brought healing and a renewed spirit. Such is the power of laughter.

As I learned to laugh at comments about my height, one of my friends learned to laugh about his lack of height. He was a wonderful after-dinner speaker as well as preacher. On one occasion at an event in Cleveland, Tennessee, he referred to me, a friend at 6'6", in one of his anecdotes. He pointed out he was more than a foot shorter than I am.

As part of his anecdote, he supposedly asked me, "How did you grow so tall?"

He related that I told him, "Just rub grease on your

belly every day."

After a considerable period of time of rubbing grease on his belly every day, he said there had been no noticeable growth.

"You have been putting me on!" he protested one day.

So I asked, "What did you use?"

"Crisco," he reported.

I answered, "You goose, everyone knows that Crisco is shortening."

Another acquaintance was moved after a long pastorate. The congregation was terribly upset because they thought the bishop had assured them of his return. But, in making the assignments for the whole conference, the pastor's unique abilities were needed elsewhere. As it so happened, this was during the "death of God" controversy at Emory University. Soon after the beloved pastor had moved, a Methodist member was complaining to the Episcopal priest about the bishop who had moved their preacher. The priest said, "Oh, cheer up. God is not dead. He's just been transferred to Johnson City."

People get restless when preachers are long-winded. During a particularly long sermon, one man got up and started to exit the sanctuary. The preacher stopped and asked the man, "Where are you going?"

"To get a haircut," the man replied.

"Why didn't you get it before you came to church?"

The man replied, "I didn't need it before I came."

Another preacher was praying over a patient in the hospital. He prayed for the patient, the church, the community, the world, and all the missionaries serving in distant places. When he finally finished and opened his eyes, the patient was gone. Summoning the nurse, he inquired about the patient. "Oh," she said, "he died while you were in China."

Preachers have to deal with lay persons who pray at great length as well. After one particularly long prayer, the preacher implored his layman: "Don't ever get that far behind with your praying again." Another pastor asked the congregation to sing hymn number 121 while the brother finished his prayer.

Every preacher has to come to terms with members who sleep during the sermon. Some are on medication, some are tired, some may be bored. One fellow told me that his sleeping demonstrated his confidence in me. One woman reported to her friend she was so embarrassed that she was not going back to church; her husband not only slept, but he snored too. Her friend reported that she had cured her husband by bringing strong Limburger cheese wrapped in a handkerchief in her purse. When he went to sleep, she rubbed the strong cheese under his nose, and he was shocked awake. Her friend decided it was worth a try. The next Sunday, early in the sermon, the man went out. The wife carefully opened her purse, removed the wrapped cheese and rubbed it under his nose. He straightened up and spoke out loudly, "Alice, wake up. You've got your feet on my pillow." Suddenly snoring didn't sound nearly so embarrassing.

District Superintendents

After serving local churches for nineteen years, I was appointed as district superintendent of the Chattanooga District. Overnight I would assume responsibility for supervising sixty-two pastoral charges with eighty local churches. Superintendents serve at the invitation of the bishop and become a part of the bishop's cabinet.

Chattanooga was an interesting mix of urban and rural churches, large and small membership churches with varied worship styles. I was inspired and challenged by the new understanding of the greatness of the Church.

The Chattanooga District had churches in three states: Tennessee, Georgia, and Alabama. Since one of a superintendent's responsibilities is to represent pastors in the appointive process, I tried to hear them all preach. With careful planning and the help of two time zones, I could sometimes slip into five services on a Sunday. After one such Sunday, I told Carolyn I was more convinced than ever that the church was of God; it could not otherwise have survived what I heard that day.

While it was certainly an honor to be chosen as a district superintendent, not everyone was pleased. My dad, himself a pastor, said he didn't raise me to be an ecclesiastical pencil pusher. An elderly member of a church I once served was bewildered that any pastor would leave her church to be a superintendent. She added that she met one of those once and was not impressed.

As you can imagine, there are some wonderful stories about superintendents. My first superintendent was Dr. Clyde Lundy. He was full of stories and mountain wisdom. One day I stopped by the district office. Dr. Lundy spotted me and invited me in for a chat. He shared his exasperation with some of the young pastors. One of them, serving out in the valley, had visited the previous week to insist that his church buy a dryer for the parsonage when they could scarcely pay his salary. So Dr. Lundy said, "Come on. I'll buy you a dryer." So, they walked downtown and purchased a hundred feet of clothesline and two dozen clothes pins.

One of the superintendent's responsibilities is to act as reconciler between pastors and congregations when there is conflict. This task becomes acute in the spring when recommendations about pastoral appointments are received. Should the pastor be returned or moved? On one occasion, I began to get phone calls. One caller said, "If you move our preacher, you will destroy our church." The next caller said, "If you don't move our preacher, you will destroy our church." In total, I received twenty-two calls—eleven for and eleven against. So I began to say to callers, "Pray for me and your church, whatever I do will be wrong."

One year, I conducted a charge conference with twelve people present representing their two churches. The next year, there were seventy very tense people present, six of those with copies of *The Book of Discipline.* They were divided over the preacher and had come to fight. Now, a part of the charge conference's responsibility is to elect officials, and at this meeting, each side had their slate of candidates. The pastor serves as chair of the nominating committee so has considerable influence over who is presented.

After delivering a brief devotion, I announced that I would not convene the conference, but we would elect a new nominating committee made up of people who could bridge their divide, and I would preside. There was no real authority for that action, but they were so relieved to avoid the anticipated fight that no one objected. Later, the new committee brought a report which was overwhelmingly adopted.

The most stressful part of being a superintendent is the making of appointments. During the spring, the bishop and cabinet would make more than a hundred appointments. To match the expectations of churches and pastors is a daunting task. Before my first experience, I asked one of the long-serving superintendents if there was anything one could do or take to make the task easier. "No," he replied. "Just be sure you have a king-size bed because the district preachers will get in and out of bed with you all night."

During the long week of projecting appointments, we would ask at breakfast, "How did you sleep?" "Like a baby" would be the reply. "That's wonderful," we would say. "No, it isn't, woke up every hour and cried."

Most of us have been blessed to have dedicated, caring administrative assistants. I was particularly blessed. When I was DS, my administrative assistant, Ethel Starnes, knew the churches and pastors and cared for them superbly. On one occasion, I was to be gone for three weeks on a mission trip. Someone asked," Who will look after the district while you are away?" My quick answer was, "The same person who looks after it while I'm here."

Sometimes superintendents and bishops are accused

of exaggerating the promise of certain appointments. One preacher asked the superintendent if he could please have a church this time around as he'd had more "possibilities" than he could stand.

An older pastor was being moved after two years. In announcing the news, the preacher said, "Well, you got what you wanted, a young preacher, and I got what I wanted, a church."

One of my tasks as a bishop was to help committees understand that they wanted an energetic preacher, not necessarily a young one. Some pastors are slow at 25; some are going strong at 65 or 70.

One of my colleagues on the cabinet was rather forthright. He went to visit a young pastor who had come from another denomination and was not accustomed to our connectional system with the supervision of pastors and shared responsibilities. The superintendent instructed him about his duties and what was expected of him. The young pastor, however, said he had been talking to the Lord that morning and the Lord told him not to do that. Quick as a flash, the superintendent said, "That's interesting. I was talking to the Lord myself this morning, and He said to tell you that you had better do that. So we have a problem here. I'm the superintendent." Suddenly the young man said, "I see what you mean."

Another pastor was keeping a large dog in the church's parsonage, and it was wreaking havoc. The superintendent instructed him to take care of the matter. When nothing had been done in a reasonable time, the superintendent called again and said, "I apparently did not explain the situation very clearly. Let me try once more. Next Monday, I will be by again. Either the dog will be gone or you will be gone." With that explanation, a remedy was found.

One superintendent in South Georgia was working with a committee to prepare them for receiving a woman pastor. The committee members assured the superintendent that they were open to the possibility of a woman pastor but not now. Suddenly a woman spoke to the man who was the main objector. "You wouldn't want Joyce P. as your pastor?" Joyce was a warm, radiant person who had preached a revival there recently. He replied, "I would love to have Joyce. I just don't want a woman." We learned to stop talking about a generic "woman," and talk about Joyce, or Mary, or whomever.

One of my favorite stories involved the rural church that got word they were to receive a woman pastor. The old boys were grumbling among themselves until one of them said, "Oh, let's treat her just like we treat our other preachers. I'll take her fishing." That calmed them down. With the late June move and heavy responsibilities of a new pastor, it was October before the fishing trip was arranged. As the wind picked up over the water, the pastor announced that she was cold and needed to return to the truck for her jacket. The old boy said that would be no problem, that he would row her back to shore. "Don't bother," she said, and she walked on the water to the shore. With that he stood up, threw his hat in the boat and said, "It's bad enough they send us a woman, but they had to send us one that can't even swim."

One of the realities of appointment-making is to find a place for every pastor in good standing. Unfortunately, some are good people but not extremely effective. We were struggling to place one fellow but had pretty much agreed on a spot in a Virginia district. The bishop asked the superintendent of that district—a most genteel, quiet man—what he thought about this appointment possibility. He quietly answered that "such an appointment was perfect if you were trying to close the church." We all applauded the reserved way he made a strong point.

A distinguished pastor was appointed as superintendent of the Valdosta District. His gifts and graces just did not fit the task, so he came off the district after one year. He was reported to have often said that he served six years on the district in that one year.

A pastor in Holston Conference was coming off the cabinet and was being roasted along with several others. The bishop stated he had worked with him for six years, and the superintendent still did not understand that before someone moved in, someone had to move out.

After three years as a superintendent, I was appointed to Munsey Memorial UMC in Johnson City, Tennessee. Munsey was a strong downtown church near the campus of East Tennessee State University. Dr. Paul Worley, who had also served Munsey at one point, was heard to say, "If I don't get to heaven, at least I got to Munsey." Indeed, Munsey and its amazing congregation were a delight to serve. In fact, I returned for an eighteen-month appointment as I was anticipating a third attempt at retirement. So now I can top Dr. Worley: If I do not get to heaven, at least I got to Munsey—twice.

After eight fulfilling years at Munsey, I was appointed to Church Street UMC in Knoxville, Tennessee. This cathedral-like structure had a magnificent musical program and attracted scores of visitors every week, so many that the staff struggled with how to follow up with all of them. I returned elated from one evening of visits in which seven persons had asked me to secure their letters of transfer to Church

Street. Every Sunday was an inspiring adventure. The sight of a large congregation, the sounds of a magnificent organ and choir, and the presence of dozens of visitors made each week memorable.

But after only thirteen months, the Southeastern Jurisdictional Conference elected me a bishop. I had mixed emotions. I had hoped to be elected but was embarrassed to be leaving a great congregation so soon. The people responded in a wonderful way, exhibiting pride that their pastor had been elected to the episcopacy. In fact, their sense of humor came through on the day of my consecration. A busload came to Lake Junaluska from Knoxville to express support wearing buttons that said, "Love 'um and leave 'um Looney" or "Landslide Looney." It takes sixty percent of the jurisdictional vote to be elected, and I was elected with just one vote to spare.

Ken Carder followed me as senior pastor to Church Street, and four years later, he too was elected a bishop. Jim Bailes, a beloved associate there, put a new quip on the church's outdoor sign, "Read my lips: no more bishops."

The Life of Bishops

I was assigned to the newly created South Georgia area and spent twelve wonderful years experiencing Southern hospitality at its best. One of South Georgia's elder statesmen attended the Jurisdictional Conference in which I was elected but left before the assignments of bishops were made. He told a good friend of mine from Holston that South Georgia would get "the runt of the litter" since it was a newly formed area and a small-membership conference. After the assignments were made, our mutual friend called to introduce the six-foot-six, 250-pound "runt" to the South Georgia member. He was horrified to discover his remark had been passed on.

Being a bishop is an awesome responsibility as one presides over the annual conference, makes the appointments with the superintendents, processes complaints or charges, counsels with pastors and churches, answers multitudes of letters and calls, and represents the larger church to the world. There are incredibly high moments as new pastors are ordained and as churches celebrate their work in the world.

There are also incredibly stressful times as pastors are assigned or disciplined, as churches complain about all sorts of issues, and as the general church conducts divisive debates about social policy and other issues. Amid it all, it is good to remember that the loving God who called and set us apart for ministry is also present to equip, sustain, and guide. It helps to keep a sense of humor too.

One of the most important tasks of the bishop is to make the annual appointments of pastors to churches, and that task gets increasingly complicated with working spouses, special medical needs, children's schools, and so on. It becomes a delicate balancing act. One spring, it seemed all of us were going through a rough time. We were making adjustments to projected appointments, hearing complaints and appeals. One bishop said, "It's a poor day when you have to appoint a pastor within driving distance of the dog's veterinarian." Another said, "I'm supposed to leave a troubled pastor in place because of season passes to the zoo."

Though a bishop's work is profoundly serious, we

cannot take ourselves too seriously. The best way to deal with the stress is to laugh at oneself as shown in some of my favorite stories involving bishops. My first bishop loved to talk about his visit to the old Centenary Church in Chattanooga. On his way to the service, he met an older woman. He helped her across the street and up the high steps to the sanctuary entrance. There she asked who was preaching today. The bishop, in his modesty said, "I understand that the bishop is," to which she replied, "Would you help me back down, please?"

One former, distinguished bishop of South Georgia was very protective of his prerogative to appoint pastors and did not respond kindly to church committees that made specific requests. Knowing this, an older woman said to him, "Bishop, if you and your cabinet, in your infinite wisdom, should return our preacher to us, we will say, 'Amen'; but, Bishop, if you and your cabinet, in your infinite wisdom, should move our preacher, we will say, 'Hallelujah'."

Another South Georgia bishop became frustrated one evening. The cabinet was trying to find a place for a pastor whom no one was eager to receive. Finally, the bishop announced that he was going for a swim and the superintendents should stay until they worked out a suitable appointment. The bishop inquired the next morning about their solution. The dean of the cabinet reported they found the ideal place for the difficult pastor: he was to be the bishop's administrative assistant. That provided a good laugh but not the solution the bishop wanted.

One of our bishops, Nolan Harmon, taught at the Candler School of Theology after his retirement. He lived to be 100, and his birthday was celebrated at Jurisdictional Conference. In his ninety-seventh year, he called Cokesbury Bookstore in Atlanta to order a new pulpit robe, and the salesclerk asked him what kind of fabric he would like. He said he wanted "durable material." On another occasion, Bishop Harmon was asked to preach at Millsaps College on the seventy-fifth anniversary of his graduation. Someone asked him how often his graduating class met. He answered that it met whenever he decided to meet with himself.

One of my Holston bishops was concerned that too many pastors were returning to a former parish to do weddings or funerals or offer inappropriate advice; thus, the newly assigned pastors were having a difficult time getting established. So, at annual conference, the bishop made a strong case for tending the current patch. "It amazes me," he said, "that some of you only become pastors to your people after you leave them. I can't forbid you from going back, but I can move you so far that it will be inconvenient."

Bishops are usually treated with so much respect that it can go to one's head. There is usually a reserved parking space, a prominent seat at the table, exaggerated words of praise and so on. One rather pompous bishop had been invited to preach in a country church, and only twelve people were in attendance. After the service, he indignantly said to the young pastor, "Did you tell them that I was coming?" The pastor replied, "I do apologize, Bishop. We tried to keep the word from getting out, but it got out anyway."

An old story is told of a haughty bishop who went with his wife for a visit in her hometown. As they were leaving, the bishop stopped to get gasoline. The attendant happened to be an old boyfriend of the wife. As they drove off, the bishop said, "Aren't you thankful you married me, otherwise you would be the wife of a service station attendant." "No," she said, "If I had married him, he would have been the bishop."

One of my favorite bishop stories in South Georgia involved a hunting dog named Preacher. There were several hunting plantations in the state, and a group of hunters from up North needed to rent a dog for their hunt. Preacher was available for $5. He was so good that they wanted him on their return the next year. As it so happened, Preacher was available, but the charge had doubled to $10. Again, the hunters returned the next year to discover that Preacher was now $100 because of the high demand. After much discussion, they decided he was certainly worth the price. The following year, they returned and asked for Preacher again. Now the price had returned to $5. What was wrong with Preacher, they wondered? They were told that nothing was really the matter. He was so good that everyone had started calling him Bishop and now all he did was sit on his tail and howl.

Holston Conference had a preacher named Ray Robinson, now deceased, who was a master of roasting people. I invited him to a church banquet, assuming he would roast some of the prominent lay persons. In fact, I sent material to help him do just that. Instead, however, he spent the evening roasting me. He began by saying that when I was born, I was so ugly my mother borrowed another baby to go to church.

Once, after an overnight visit, Ray informed me that he wanted me to help with his funeral. Not knowing what might be coming, I replied, "I don't know what to say." Ray replied, "I want you to buy the casket."

His reputation was so well known that he became a fixture in honoring (roasting) our retiring or visiting bishops. During one roast, Ray stated that our retiring bishop was loved all over Holston Conference: there was a couple in Chattanooga, one in Knoxville, and two couples up in Virginia. Ray insisted that the bishop was also an eloquent preacher. He further explained he had, in fact, heard the bishop thirty-four times and both sermons were good.

When one bishop left Holston for another conference, more than a dozen pastors transferred from Holston to that conference. The bishop was asked to take our greetings to each one of those pastors by name. Then the comment was made that he effected more moves in Holston after he left than he did while he was here. As everyone howled, including the bishop, the roaster commented that the bishop would rob a dead fly from a blind spider. Another bishop gave a series of lectures on the Old Testament. The comment was made that we now knew what it was to be slain by the jawbone of an ass.

Most who knew Ray Robinson loved him and appreciated his sharp humor. His funeral service was packed to overflowing. I later commented to his wife that it was amazing to see such an outpouring of love since most of us had been "insulted" by him at one time or another.

Annual Conference

One of the responsibilities of a resident bishop is to preside over the annual conference(s) of the area. As the name indicates, this meeting of delegates occurs yearly and is made up of lay and clergy representatives from each local church. Budgets are adopted, conference leaders are elected, credentials for ministry are granted, social-issue resolutions are considered, and pastors' appointments are announced. Throughout the four-day conference, there are reports of mission accomplishments and powerful services of worship.

Presiding is always a challenge but, for me, very fulfilling. The presider is to enable the delegates to do their work, not to exert one's own wishes. This also involves moving the agenda along without rushing it unnecessarily. Some presenters had to be reminded to summarize their presentations since the delegates had already received written copies. A gentle reminder to be brief was sometimes heeded but not always.

The service of ordination and the reading of appointments were high moments in every gathering. The liturgy for ordination never ceased to touch something deep within and reminded me of my own ordination. The responsibility to care for God's flock feels overwhelming, and the responsibility of matching pastors with churches seemed to get heavier with each appointment season.

Our United Methodist Committee on Relief is involved in ways beyond imagination wherever disaster strikes. I observed this firsthand while serving in South Georgia where we had two devastating floods in four years. When most other agencies had moved on, UMCOR's work continued.

Before 1988, the South Georgia Conference was a part of the Atlanta episcopal area. South Georgia had shared a bishop—who resided in Atlanta—with the North Georgia Conference. With twenty-one districts and more than 400,000 members, the bishop was not often seen in local churches or charges.

One of my goals as the new bishop in South Georgia was to be as visible as possible. With only nine districts and 140,000 members, that became a realistic possibility. To that end, I assigned four Sundays each year to the respective districts. The superintendents were to schedule three appearances for the day.

By the end of eight years, I had visited each charge, either to preach or share in some service of dedication.

The results were most positive. It was reported that I was the first bishop to visit since Francis Asbury, or the first bishop to visit in fifty years, or the first bishop ever to visit. By the end of twelve years, I was proud to have visited more than once in forty percent of the charges.

At one point, I scheduled a visit to one of our strong churches in a county seat town—for the third time. It was announced in the weekly newsletter, however, that this was the first visit of a bishop in twenty years (not the third in twelve)! Apparently, my presence had not made the impression that I had assumed, but they made an impression on me.

I met so many dedicated lay and clergy persons who exhibited the spirit of Christ, and I witnessed the difference so many local churches made in their communities. The Church is so much greater than even the sum of its parts.

One evening I visited a small local church. One of the lay leaders greeted me with a smile saying, "We aren't particularly impressed by having a bishop visit." Not being sure where this was heading, I said I understood. He then introduced me to four families whose last name was Bishop, and the church treasurer who was a Pope. We had a good laugh, and I was reminded how insignificant our cherished titles can be.

Another small-membership church picked up on one of my family stories and raised $1,400 by collecting aluminum cans for the Children's Home in Macon, Georgia. On my first visit with Mom and Dad after being elected a bishop, Dad let me know that, even as a bishop, I was still his boy and I would do as I was told—there was no doubt in my mind about that. I was then instructed to fill a garbage bag with aluminum cans from the ditches around Emory, Virginia. The reason for this assignment was my parents' deep commitment to mission projects. The collected cans, the produce and homemade jellies sold, and the like had inspired others to give. During their retirement, Mom and Dad raised more than a million dollars and left a sizable amount to the conference for continuing support of projects. Thinking that the people in South Georgia would get a kick out of their bishop picking up cans inspired other projects.

National figures like Roslyn Carter and Millard Fuller reminded us of our social responsibilities; global church leaders shared the wonder of the universal gospel and demonstrated our common humanity. An African bishop spoke on the commission given by

Christ to make disciples of all nations. He urged us to do more "than fish out of some other's bucket." This was a clever reminder that we gain most of our new members by transfer from other churches rather than professions of faith.

For more than 200 years, Methodist conferences have begun by singing the words of Charles Wesley's hymn:

And are we yet alive, and see each other's face? Glory and thanks to Jesus give, for His almighty grace.

This stirring hymn reminds us of the faith of those who have come before us and brings hope as we look ahead.

General Conference

The United Methodist Church holds a General Conference every four years. Delegates from Asia, Africa, Europe, and North America convene to set budgets, debate social issues, report on mission accomplishments, amend *The Book of Discipline*, and participate in worship. The display of national dress and culture is inspiring.

One delegate had a unique way of calling for the previous question when debate needed to end. He would say, "We have other fish to fry," or, "We have more corn to shuck," or "We have more hay to bale." His unending supply of quips brought needed relief to the entire conference.

It has been a privilege to participate in the last ten General Conferences. We have had—and will continue to have—our divisive debates, and our unity is fragile. However, we celebrate the strength of "the Connection" whereby we are able to do so much more together than we could do alone.

The number of delegates is so large that it is often difficult to get the attention of the presiding officer in order to speak, especially from the back of the venue. One delegate on the back row resorted to mounting his table to wave a red flag tied to a broom handle. He was recognized!

During one General Conference, there was a debate over inclusive language in the Discipline regarding the Trinitarian formula. A legislative committee was proposing that the Trinitarian formula—"Father, Son, and Holy Spirit"—be changed to "Creator, Redeemer, Sustainer." During passionate speeches, a delegate gave a three-sentence summary of his feelings: "Anyone who does not know that our Lord taught us to say 'Our Father' is ignorant. Anyone who thinks they know better than our Lord is arrogant. Anyone who is both ignorant and arrogant should not even be a delegate to this General Conference." Both sides of the argument enjoyed his lighthearted summary.

On another divisive issue, a well-known delegate began an impassioned speech. He was primed and ready to go, just not on the matter at hand. He delivered his speech with such ardor that the presiding officer could not interrupt him soon enough.

Finally, the presiding officer asked, "Brother, are we

talking about the same matter?" Realizing that he had "jumped the gun," he apologized and returned to his seat. A friend whispered as he passed, "You can go back to sleep now."

Foundation for Evangelism

After retirement from the episcopacy, I worked
for eight years with the Foundation for Evangelism.
The foundation's primary goal was to raise funds
to provide a professor of evangelism for United
Methodist seminaries located in the United
States, Germany, Africa, and Russia. The trustees
represented exceptional lay persons from throughout
the connection. In my role as a staff person, I was
privileged to present our work across the denomination
and enjoy some remarkable experiences.

The United Methodist Church in Oblong, Illinois,
invited me to preach for a series of community services
at a town venue, hoping to reach persons who would
not normally visit a church building. The community
was still talking about a wedding announcement in the
local paper.

The headline read:

Oblong Girl Marries Normal Boy

Normal, Illinois, was a nearby town.

On another occasion, I was invited to preach in New Haven, Connecticut. They set up a tent in a parking lot to attract outsiders, and during the service, walkers-by would occasionally pause to hear a bit of the service. I was curious to learn about this unusual revival setting in Connecticut. Upon inquiry, I learned that the new chair of evangelism had recently moved from South Carolina and had suggested they try a Southern tradition. The results were disappointing, but the effort was commendable.

In a visit to Alaska, I met a retired pastor who used his wood-carving skills to craft totem poles as a Christian witness. The story of Christ was told using Native symbols such as bears, eagles, and so on. The interpretation was inspiring and instructive, and a miniature totem pole was given as a gift to the foundation.

On another occasion, I was to speak in a Kentucky church. The sermon dealt with the humor of Jesus and our need to become the kind of Christians who could laugh at ourselves and with other people. I had borrowed the title, "Holy Hilarity." During the sermon, the elderly church pianist left the piano to sit with an equally aged friend on the front row. They apparently thought that humor was inappropriate in the sacred space for not even a smile crossed their faces. Humor needs a response, but they were killing me. The temptation to invite them to move to the back had to be resisted.

The Foundation for Evangelism's ministry is of such import that it receives my continued support and involvement. Organized in 1949 by Dr. Harry Denman to provide resources for the Church's task of evangelism, it continues as "a catalyst to equip disciples to share the Good News of Jesus Christ."

In recent years, a large focus has been to partner with United Methodist seminaries in providing a professor of evangelism. As these professors train hundreds of students and equip them to share their faith, the foundation's influence accelerates, and the cause of sensible evangelism multiplies. To date, this partnership includes thirteen seminaries: ten in the United States and one each in Zimbabwe, Africa, Russia, and Germany. The professorships are named for the famed missionary leader E. Stanley Jones.

In addition to grants for promising new ministries, the foundation annually recognizes lay, clergy, and youth evangelists from participating annual conferences. These Harry Denman Awards give recognition to an amazing variety of faith-sharing methods and inspire others to find their own way to share the Good News.

The Church Universal

Christians around the world share much in common, though we tend to emphasize our differences. My own faith has been enriched by persons of different persuasions. I graduated from a United Methodist seminary, but I have done additional studies in Presbyterian and Lutheran seminaries. Great preachers from a variety of denominations have inspired my learning and preaching. Participation in the Tri-Cities (East Tennessee) Preaching Mission introduced me to many of the noted preachers of America.

It was a privilege to be part of an ongoing dialogue between the Methodist and Roman Catholic world churches. There were eight representatives from each body who would spend five years together in each cycle. The cycle in which I was a participant explored how we could speak the truth in love. We recognized our differences but embraced what we held in common.

During our dialogue, we met in Paris and Venice and were lodged in a Catholic convent; in Jerusalem, we were housed in a Catholic hotel; and at St. Simons, Georgia, we stayed at the United Methodist Retreat Center.

What a gift to be reminded that the Christian faith is so much greater than any singular expression of it and that the body of Christ embraces the world. From Australia, the Philippines, the Vatican, France, England, Ireland, the United States of America, and South Africa, we discovered new brothers and sisters in Christ.

On one occasion, I participated in the consecration service for the new Episcopal bishop of Georgia. To accommodate the expected crowd, the Catholic cathedral was used as the venue. I felt a bit out of place in a high church service in such an awesome cathedral, but I felt very much at home when John and Charles Wesley were listed among the Episcopal saints being remembered. John and Charles came to the New World as Anglican clergymen, and Charles was the first rector of the Anglican church on St. Simons.

When the World Methodist Conference meets every five years, we recognize the ecumenical dignitaries in attendance. One year the introductions had a beautiful flavor: a Catholic bishop (our grandmother), an Anglican bishop (our mother), and a Salvation Army general (our offspring).

Not only do our denominations share much in common, but so do our cultures. It has been amazing to see how the Good News of God's love connects to human longing across the globe. While preaching in Asia, Africa, Europe, Latin America, and the USA, the response has been remarkably similar. One realizes that we are one family. We speak different languages, live in varied cultures, but we are all loved and claimed by the same God.

The pageantry of a World Methodist gathering almost leads one to an involuntary gasp. As each country's delegation moves in procession with their banners and native dress, one can only celebrate such diversity. The colorful dress from Africa, Asia, and the Pacific Islands makes our business garb seem drab and colorless. The tapestry we offer together is so much more remarkable than anything created by uniformity.

Outside the Church Walls

While still in my forties, I was appointed to Munsey
Memorial in Johnson City, Tennessee, a wonderful
church with many members, a great music program,
and a large staff. The pastor who preceded me was
more experienced and better known, and it was a bit
intimidating. On the first Sunday, I stood in the high
pulpit and looked out at a crowded sanctuary. I said,
"If I had any sense, I would be scared to death," and I
reminded them of the previous pastors. At the end of
the service, a local funeral director shook my hand and
said, "Relax, boy. We don't let our preachers fail." Who
can count the number of wonderful people who are just
like that?

Led by lay volunteers, the presence of God is
experienced in many ministries outside the "normal"
church programs. In one such program at Munsey
Memorial, the homeless and street people are welcomed

for food and fellowship during the week and for worship on Sunday. The fellowship enjoyed in the worship experience mirrors that of the early church. Street people mingle with university professors, business leaders, and volunteers. The heartfelt love and care among them is truly inspiring, a foretaste of eternity.

At Munsey Memorial, lay volunteers regularly visit a penal institution in a neighboring county. They bring treats, lead Bible studies, and interact with the inmates. The highlight of the year is a big Christmas party followed by Holy Communion. I was privileged to share in this special service one year. Earlier in the evening, I visited with men who were serving life sentences with no prospect for early release. There was an overwhelming sense of God's love and presence as we shared the bread and juice. Do this in remembrance of me and receive unmerited love and forgiveness. These men were locked away by society but not from the care of the Christian community nor the presence of God.

In retirement, I served for a period as pastor of a small-membership church, Telford UMC, in Telford, Tennessee. Their men's group built ramps for people who could not manage steps and provided bicycles for children whose parents could not afford them. The group realized that such services could be done by all and became inclusive of women and youth. The special

joy of these associations around hammer and saw will
not be forgotten. As a follower of Jesus, the carpenter of
Nazareth, it has been a great privilege to offer my hands
and body as well as my voice in service and mission.

Headquartered in Americus, Georgia, Habitat for
Humanity is an organization that brings together
people from all faiths to build affordable housing. While
serving in South Georgia, I met the founder, Millard
Fuller, and participated in a weekend blitz to build
twenty houses. The goal was to eventually replace all
substandard housing in the county. Two of Habitat's best
supporters happened to be President and Mrs. Jimmy
Carter, who lived in an adjacent county. Meeting the
needs of the poor and forgotten bridges all our artificial
divisions. "Inasmuch as ye have done it unto one of the
least of these, ye have done it unto me," said Jesus.

Carolyn and I enjoyed lunch with the Carters on
another occasion in Plains, their hometown. President
Carter has an amazing grasp of Christian theology and
teaches a Sunday school class attended by people from
across the world. During our time together, President
Carter shared a story from Tolstoy that I had never
heard: "A bishop was on a trip by boat in the Pacific.
He asked about a small island in the distance. It was
reported that there was nothing of interest there, only
a few hermits. The bishop insisted on being brought

ashore. Upon learning that they did not know the Lord's Prayer, he spent the day teaching them the words and proper use.

"As they were sailing away, they heard a strange sound. The hermits were running on the water and shouting, 'Wait! We have forgotten the words!' The bishop, having noted they were running on the water, replied, 'I believe you know all you need to know about prayer.'"

One year, the Albany area of South Georgia was covered by a 500-year flood. Caskets were washed out of the ground, roads were gutted, businesses and homes were destroyed. As a conference, we felt overwhelmed. However, the United Methodist Church, other denominations, and agencies sprang into action. Our own relief agency provided a volunteer who helped open a huge warehouse, gave grants to help hire staff and purchase materials, and provided hundreds of volunteers. While many organizations left in a few weeks, the conference work continued for years, thanks to the connection we share as United Methodists.

We experience real tension trying to hold together such a diverse, worldwide organization; but, in times of crisis, we see its value. One week, a small group of us worked to rebuild a severely damaged house. The widow, who lived there alone, had given her life savings to a contractor for the job, and he disappeared

with her money. Later, I received a moving letter from
the lady. After losing her savings, she explained in
the letter, she had lost her faith in humanity and even
in God, but now all was restored as she had been
visited by "a cloud of angels." We were warmed by
the gracious letter but amused by the description of
our motley crew as "angels." We were quite a sight:
a bishop, nine superintendents, and members of the
conference staff. The pastors of the conference would
have been horrified to have seen us.

Staff

Some of the most inspiring persons I have met were staff members. Their talent, dedication, and support were invaluable. In the early 1960s, I was appointed to Baker's Chapel, which later became Pleasant View in Virginia. On the first Sunday, I noticed in the choir a distinguished gentleman who looked like a state senator. To my amazement, he was the part-time custodian and school bus driver. He brought such care and dignity to the task that we renamed his position "maintenance engineer." The building glowed under his care; he cared not for a building but for the House of God.

During my first meeting with members of the staff parish committee in my fourth appointment, Broad Street in Cleveland, Tennessee, we were discussing their expectations for my ministry. They suggested that my most important job was to keep Crill and Horace happy; ministers could come and go, but they could not do without these two. Horace was the custodian. Every Sunday, the floors shined and everything was spotless and in order. He moved about the building with a cloth draped on his arm as if to say, "Is there anything I can do to help you?"

Crill led the church choir and directed the high school band. Of 900 students, 300 were in the band. Many people attended the football games to hear the band. Crill's wife was the church organist and likewise gifted. Their music was an offering to God, not a performance. And, in so many places, the musicians are vital leaders in making worship uplifting and joyous.

My appreciation for church secretaries and administrative assistants knows no bounds. In my first two appointments, I served as pastor and secretary. Typing and reproduction of the bulletin, answering the phone, sending letters, and producing newsletters were all my responsibility. Fortunately, I had learned to type and cut stencils in high school.

After eleven years, those tasks could be handled by someone more skilled and creative, for such persons set the tone for people who called. They answered questions, directed persons to the right resources, and occasionally gave spiritual encouragement. They often knew the congregation and individual parishioners better than the minister. In truth, they were esteemed colleagues in ministry.

How many times have these servants of God diffused an explosive situation or offered help and encouragement? When serving as superintendent, I would occasionally call one church office just to hear the secretary answer the phone: "Hello, this is _____. May I help you?" It was said in such a lilting, uplifting way, I was tempted to say, "You have, thank you."

Overseas

We often fail to realize that the hospitality we offer to strangers has eternal consequences. When the Holston Conference sent a short-term mission team to Liberia, West Africa, I was paired with Doug Smith and sent to Zwedru, a remote town in logging country. We landed on a dirt airstrip and prayed that an early rain wouldn't strand us. While arrangements were being made for our lodging, we were cared for by the village chief.

His story was fascinating and inspiring. As a boy, he had a deep thirst for education. After exhausting the opportunities in the small village, he made a several-hundred-mile trip on foot to Monrovia. Upon completion of what education was available there, he managed to travel to the United States, specifically the state of Kansas.

He shared that, early in his studies, he visited a small

Methodist church, and even in those early days of the
Civil Rights movement, the congregation welcomed him
warmly. Their friendship led him to become a practicing
Christian. After returning to Liberia, he taught others
and then served as the respected chief in Zwedru. If he
had not been treated as one of God's children in Kansas,
who might have welcomed us in Liberia?

Years later, I heard a similar story when visiting
a church in Estonia. The country had been brutally
overrun by the Soviet Union; Estonia's resources were
plundered and the Church suppressed. A small church
in Tallin, however, had managed to survive. After
regaining freedom, the Estonian congregation grew in
strength. Incidentally, Russian families continued to
visit the city to enjoy the beaches.

One day, a young Russian teen slipped into one of the
services and sat near the back. He was a strange sight
with dyed hair and torn clothes. An elderly woman
made her way to him. He assumed that she was going
to invite him to leave, but instead, she invited him
to come forward and share her hymnal. The friendly
welcome touched him, and each year when the family
visited, he returned for the services. He began to
smuggle Bibles into Russia and became part of a small
Christian cell that met regularly to study the Bible.
Occasionally, he even led the group. When I heard

the story, this man was pastor of the largest United Methodist congregation in Russia. Again, a small courtesy had eternal consequences.

During the visit to Estonia, I served as the representative for the Council of Bishops at a meeting of the Central Conference for Northern Europe. One of the meeting's highlights was the recognition of the move of the Russian Annual Conference from provisional to full status. The Methodist Church had been eliminated under Soviet Communism but had now grown to the point of being a full conference with the establishment of a new seminary. With this recognition, their brothers and sisters from the host conference of Estonia welcomed them with open arms and warm hearts. Surely, in Christ, there is no East or West but one great fellowship of love throughout the whole wide earth.

On an episcopal visit to Russia, I spent some time in Moscow and St. Petersburg. The Methodist Church, which had been outlawed under communism, was beginning to grow. A missionary from my home conference was serving in the St. Petersburg area, so one evening we had dinner in the home of a lay leader from a small congregation in the city. Interestingly, the lay leader had been a high official in the communist party before becoming a United Methodist. The skills she learned there were now used in her leadership in the church. Every week, she called each family of this hundred-member congregation to remind them of church programs and to ask about any pastoral needs. God continues to work in transformative ways with unlikely people.

Two World Leaders in Evangelism

In addition to my dad, who was a compelling preacher and effective personal evangelist, I was mentored and inspired by the writing and example of Harry Denman and Sir Alan Walker. Dr. Denman headed the Board of Evangelism for the Methodist Church. As a layman, he was a powerful preacher and a most sensitive personal evangelist. He lived very simply. In traveling the world for the Church, he often had difficulty clearing customs: there was something suspicious about an American who had only a change of underwear and shirt. Friends would give him a new coat or suit only to see it on a homeless person within days.

Denman had a special concern for people he met in restaurants, hotels, or public transport. They were often shocked when he asked them to pray for him. Instead, they would ask him for his prayers. He had a natural way to learn about people's circumstances and offer a meaningful prayer. Before departing, he would get their addresses and follow up with a personal word of encouragement and a book or pamphlet to guide their spiritual journey. Nearly all of his secretary's time was given to such correspondence. My wife, Carolyn, sat with him once and asked for counsel about a spiritual struggle. He listened, offered a helpful prayer, and followed up with a personal letter and helpful booklet.

On one occasion, Denman was to lead a week of special services in a local church. The pastor went to the train station to pick him up during the early afternoon, but he was nowhere to be found. The pastor spent a frantic afternoon wondering where he might be. The service began without a speaker, but Dr. Denman appeared just in time. Before beginning to speak, he asked, "How many of you are here because I invited you?" About a third of the large congregation raised their hand. He had exited the train on the other side of the track and had spent the afternoon visiting from house to house. With Dr. Denman, love and friendship were more persuasive than pressure.

Sir Alan Walker led the Central Mission of the Methodist Church in Sydney, Australia, and eventually became director of World Evangelism for the Global Methodist Church. I met him through his writings, world preaching missions that he led, and in his home in Sydney.

When the Central Mission's building burned, Sir Alan Walker led the church to replace the ruined building with a movie theater. He knew that the outsider would more likely feel comfortable in such a building. So, the new building had a dual purpose: entertainment and worship. This unique ministry thrived. The mission developed outreach ministries for seniors, at-risk teens, and the homeless. They developed a crisis telephone ministry with trained lay volunteers that was so successful that it was adopted in the USA under the name Contact. I profited greatly from the six months of training before becoming a counselor.

Walker made such a contribution to the well-being of the world that he was knighted by the Queen of England. Through World Evangelism, he became the best-known Methodist in the world. His passion was always for the outsider. The Gospel, he knew, was intended for the whole world, especially the forgotten and marginalized, and he understood clearly that society needed transforming as well.

While living in Johnson City, Tennessee, I was able to schedule Sir Alan to be the speaker for the Johnson City Preaching Mission in an event that brought together most denominations in the area. Walker wanted the services to be held in a school or public hall; the committee, however, chose the large, centrally located United Methodist Church downtown. To say the least, Sir Alan was not pleased. "Well," he said, "we will have a good church meeting but not a mission." In every service, he constructively challenged us regarding our faith and responsibility for the sensitive social issues that faced us.

Inspiring Lay Members

Not only are people funny, but they are also inspiring
in many ways. I could never be thankful enough for
the way my own life has been enriched by the support,
encouragement, example, and prayers of lay people.
In my first appointment on the Rising Fawn Circuit, I
met a beautiful older woman who had a quiet radiance
and wisdom. She had only finished the fifth grade, but
her understanding of God was beyond imagining. She
studied and prayed regularly and had a relationship
with God that was personal and intimate. When she
prayed aloud, one was tempted to look up to see this
"friend" with whom she conversed. When a board
meeting became tense, she would listen carefully and
then say gently, "Have you thought of this?" What she
asked was so sensible that we wanted to say, "No, but
why didn't we?" The tension evaporated.

I remember a distinguished man who was the town

postmaster and church lay leader. As a young man, he had lost his left arm at the shoulder in an industrial accident. With only one arm, he had become an excellent golfer and exceptional hunter. Younger men who accompanied him had to work hard to keep from being embarrassed. His leadership in the county and local church was even more remarkable. He encouraged the best and offered support generously.

Once this gentleman's church asked him to lead an effort to redecorate the sanctuary. He asked for suggestions on color scheme, and everyone had a different color in mind. With no agreement possible, he called an interior decorator from the city and followed her recommendations. It was a beautiful matching of the wall colors and dominant colors of the stained glass windows. The whole atmosphere of the sanctuary glowed with a new radiance. Of course, one comment from another man on the first Sunday illustrates the impossibility of pleasing everyone. "Hmm," he said, "looks like a dance hall."

Retirement

After four failed attempts at retirement, I am now enjoying the first extended time without employment. Retirement brings an opportunity to relax and pursue neglected interests and hobbies, but it also brings a new awareness of human limitations and bodily deterioration. I asked an old man once how he was doing. He replied that he was doing great for the shape he was in.

It is important to learn to celebrate what one can do rather than bemoan what one cannot do. My running days are past, but my walking and hiking days bring great reward. I am particularly grateful for the gift of cataract surgery. Night driving was becoming a hazard, but surgery that removed the cataracts brought better sight than experienced since teen years.

What a joy to have hearing aids! One elderly man

became convinced that his wife was going deaf, but she wouldn't agree to see a doctor. Finally, he went himself and described the wife's problem. When the doctor asked just how severe the loss was, the man replied that he had no way of knowing. So, the man was told to speak to his wife from varying distances to get an indication of the severity. Upon his arrival back home, he called out from the front door, "Honey, what's for supper?" When there was no answer, he went to the living room and repeated the question. When there was no answer, he tried again from the den. Again, there was no answer. So, he went very close to her in the kitchen. "Honey, what's for supper?" whereupon she said, "Are you deaf? I already told you three times!"

Another man had purchased an expensive pair of hearing aids and was asked how he liked them. He replied that they were wonderful and that he was hearing things that he had not heard in years. "Well, how does your family feel about your improved hearing?" "Oh, I haven't told them yet. I've had to change my will six times already."

United Methodists love to gather around fellowship meals. One of my Baptist friends teases me by saying that we must believe in "salvation by grease."

A pastor was visiting one of his church members who had celebrated her 103rd birthday. During the conversation, she announced that she could now die in peace. Interested in her reasoning, he asked, "What happened?" She replied that she had been able to place the last of her children in the nursing home.

Two elderly men were talking about their memory problems. One announced he was taking a course at the community center which had helped his memory tremendously. His friend immediately asked the name of the course since he needed help with his memory as well. The gentleman began to ponder, "What is the name of that course? What is the name of that course?" Finally, he said, "What is the name of that thing with a long stem and thorns?" "A rose," the other man answered. "That's it!" Then he called out to his wife, "Rose, what's the name of that course I'm taking?"

Art Linkletter, the famous TV personality, wanted to do some community service. Someone suggested the folks at the nursing home would love to see him. So, with delighted satisfaction, he showed up at a local facility. Seeing an older woman standing in the public area, he went over and said, "Do you know who I am?" She answered, "No, I'm sorry, but the lady at the desk should be able to tell you."

Intending to practice his call to evangelism, a young man asked an older woman if she was ready for the hereafter. She replied, "Oh, sonny, I live in the hereafter. I go into the kitchen, the living room, the bedroom and say, 'What am I here after?'"

The Renewing Power
of Laughter

We are all aware of the renewing power of laughter. It is good for your health. It knits friends together and can relieve tense situations. The ability to laugh at oneself is a sign of genuine maturity. And what if God laughs— not at us but with us? Would that not make a profound difference in our understanding and relationship?

Some years ago, I came to my office on Monday morning feeling good about what had happened on Sunday. The sermon had been well received with a warm response. At that time, I was also functioning as the church secretary, so I was alone in the office. In this mood of self-congratulation, I suddenly realized, to my shame, that I was on an ego trip. Normally, I would have bowed my head and said, "God, forgive me, this is terrible. This is unbecoming for a Christian and doubly so for a minister."

But instead, I sat up straight and spoke out loud, "You have a charmer on your hands, Father." In that moment, I sensed that God laughed. I cannot prove that or explain it, but in that moment, there was warmth, understanding, and acceptance. A parent and child laughed together. My heart was strangely warmed. What I had been preaching now made deep personal sense.

God knows all about us—our failures, our pain, our struggles—and God loves us still. We can love such a God and even laugh together. After all, Jesus did come to give us life and life abundant. He came to teach us God's way so that our joy may be full.

Laugh on, dear friends!

Made in the USA
Coppell, TX
09 June 2022

78656569R00095